交通信息感知理论与方法

THEORY AND METHOD OF TRANSPORTATION INFORMATION PERCEPTION

赵池航　连　捷　党　倩　著

东南大学出版社
·南京·

内 容 简 介

本书分上、下两篇,上篇用中文撰写,下篇用英文撰写。本书以交通信息感知理论与方法为主线,系统研究了交通场景中驾驶人—车辆—路面信息的感知及获取有关理论与技术,主要包括:①交通场景中车辆区域检测、车辆品牌特征提取及识别的理论与方法;②路面破损检测、特征提取及识别的理论与方法;③驾驶人脸部区域检测、疲劳特征提取及识别的理论与方法;④驾驶人姿态的特征提取及识别的理论与方法。

本书可作为交通信息工程与控制、交通安全工程和载运工具运用工程等专业研究生的教材,也可以作为高等院校、科研院所和企事业单位从事智能交通行业工程技术人员的参考书。

图书在版编目(CIP)数据

交通信息感知理论与方法:汉,英/赵池航,连捷,党倩著. —南京:东南大学出版社,2014.9
 ISBN 978-7-5641-5111-9

Ⅰ.①交⋯ Ⅱ.①赵⋯ ②连⋯ ③党⋯ Ⅲ.①交通信息系统—研究—汉、英 Ⅳ.①U49

中国版本图书馆 CIP 数据核字(2014)第 177321 号

交通信息感知理论与方法

出版发行	东南大学出版社	
社　　址	南京市四牌楼2号　邮编 210096	
出 版 人	江建中	
网　　址	http://www.seupress.com	
电子邮箱	press@seupress.com	
经　　销	全国各地新华书店	
印　　刷	南京玉河印刷厂	
开　　本	787mm×1092mm　1/16	
印　　张	7.25	
字　　数	176 千	
版　　次	2014 年 9 月第 1 版	
印　　次	2014 年 9 月第 1 次印刷	
书　　号	ISBN 978-7-5641-5111-9	
定　　价	24.00 元	

本社图书若有印装质量问题,请直接与营销部联系。电话(传真):025-83791830

前　言

随着国民经济的快速增长,交通运输事业在我国国民经济和居民生活中的地位也逐步提高,人—车—路信息感知技术的研究已经成为智能交通系统中最重要的研究课题。计算机图像处理技术、通信与网络传输技术及电子技术的发展使得交通的智能化及现代化管理和控制成为可能,通过建立交通智能管理和控制体系,综合管理及控制人、车和路等交通参与体,对于提高交通运输效率和效益,保证交通安全,促进可持续发展具有十分重要的作用。全球范围内每年度的关于交通事故的统计报告表明,大量交通事故是由人为因素引起的,自动理解和识别驾驶员疲劳及异常行为可有效地降低由人为引起的交通事故率;车辆区域检测及定位是智能交通系统中车辆实时追踪、车辆类型识别及分类等应用领域的基础;而车辆类型识别技术能够在套牌车辆自动识别、交通监控场景车型自动统计分析等领域发挥重要作用;公路路面破损严重影响了道路交通的安全性和舒适性,基于线阵图像的路面破损检测及识别能够快速准确地进行公路路况的评价。本书共6章,分上、下两篇,上篇用中文撰写,下篇用英文撰写,主要的研究工作包括如下几个方面:

第一章主要论述了国内外交通环境中车辆与路面信息感知技术的研究现状及趋势。

第二章主要研究了静态图像中车辆区域定位技术及车辆品牌识别技术。首先,提出了一种基于车辆轮廓对称特征和车牌对称特征的两种特征融合的车辆检测方法,并与基于车辆边缘、车牌、车辆纹理特征和车辆图像Gabor特征等5种检测方法进行了对比分析,通过实验验证了所提出的基于对称特征融合车辆区域检测方法的有效性;其次,提出了一种采用两种不同的特征融合互补形成新的特征以进一步提高识别率的方法,并对特征进行主成分分析(PCA)以实现数据降维,在保持分类性能的同时提高了分类效率,通过实验验证了所提出的算法的有效性;最后,本文提出了一种带有"拒识"功能的高可靠性级联集成分类器方法,级联集成分类器的第一级包含朴素贝叶斯分类器、k-近邻、多层神经网络和支持向量机,通过将被第一级"拒识"的样本送入第二级集成分类器进行识别提升可靠性,第二级集成分类器是使用多层神经网络作为基分类器并结合旋转森林的元学习方法实现,通过对18种类型车辆超过4 000张输入样本的测试实验验证了本文方法的有效性。

第三章基于线阵CCD路面图像,研究了路面破损的检测及分类方法。首先,针对路面破损图像中破损像素较正常路面像素灰度较低这一基本特征,对比分析了领域灰度差分法、局部灰度最小分析法和分块标记法的优势和弱点,基于级联分类器的思想,提出了用于路面破损检测的联合检测器,理论分析和实验结果表明联合检测器的性能优于领域灰度差分法、局部灰度最小分析法和分块标记法,其检测率达到96.7%;其次,研究了路面破损图像的特征提取及分类方法,提出将Contourlet变换用于路面破损特征提取,并对比分析了Contourlet变换、边缘方向直方图、方向梯度直方图和分层梯度方向直方图四种特征提取方法,基于构建的东南大学路面破损图像数据库,采用支持向量机(Support Vector Machines, SVMs)分类器对提取的4种特征进行了对比实验,实验结果表明Contourlet特征提取方法优于其他3种方法;最后,提出了一种基于联合特征及随机子空间交叉内核支持向量机分类器集成的路面破损自动化分类方法,研究了图像联合特征的融合策略,利用串行融合策略构造了路面破损图像的Contourlet变换和EOH联合特征,并基于分类器集成的构造原则实现了交叉内核支持向量机分类器的集成方案,采用东南大学路面图像数据库进行了实验,实验结果表明Contourlet变换和EOH联合特征及随机子空间交叉内核支持向量机分类器集成优于单一Contoulet变换特征和EOH特征。

第四章主要论述了国内外交通场景中驾驶人疲劳和异常姿态信息感知技术的研究现状及趋势。

第五章研究了基于Curvelet变换的驾驶人疲劳等级感知技术。首先,构建了东南大学驾驶人疲劳等级数据库;其次,提出将Curvelet变换应用于驾驶人疲劳特征提取,并采用支持向量机作为分类器,与线性神经网络、k-近邻、多层神经网络和Parzen进行了对比实验,实验结果证明了所提出方法的有效性。

第六章研究了基于Nonsubsampled Contourlet变换的驾驶人异常行为感知技术。首先,构建了东南大学驾驶人姿态数据库;其次,提出将Nonsubsampled Contourlet变换用于驾驶人姿态特征提取,并采用k-近邻作为分类器,与加性交叉核向量机、多层神经网络和Parzen分类器进行了对比实验,实验结果证明了所提出方法的有效性。

作 者

2014年6月

目 录

上篇 车辆及路面信息感知

第一章 国内外的发展及研究现状 ………………………………………… 3
1.1 车辆信息感知的研究现状 …………………………………………… 3
1.1.1 车辆区域检测方法研究现状 …………………………………… 4
1.1.2 车辆品牌及型号识别研究现状 ………………………………… 5
1.2 公路路面信息感知的研究现状 ……………………………………… 7
1.2.1 路面图像预处理技术现状 ……………………………………… 8
1.2.2 路面破损检测技术研究现状 …………………………………… 9
1.2.3 路面破损分类技术研究现状 …………………………………… 10

第二章 车辆信息感知理论与技术 ……………………………………… 12
2.1 车辆图像采集及车辆目标区域检测 ………………………………… 13
2.1.1 基于对称特征的车辆检测方法 ………………………………… 14
2.1.2 其他车辆检测方法 ……………………………………………… 17
2.1.3 感兴趣区域(ROI)定位 ………………………………………… 19
2.2 特征描述器 …………………………………………………………… 21
2.2.1 梯度方向直方图(HOG) ………………………………………… 21
2.2.2 Contourlet 变换 ………………………………………………… 21
2.2.3 特征降维 ………………………………………………………… 23
2.2.4 组合特征及降维 ………………………………………………… 24
2.3 基于级联集成分类器的可靠分类 …………………………………… 25
2.4 实验分析 ……………………………………………………………… 34

2.4.1 单个分类器实验 ………………………………………………… 35
2.4.2 级联集成分类器实验 …………………………………………… 37
2.5 小结 ……………………………………………………………………… 40

第三章 路面信息感知理论与技术 …………………………………………… 42

3.1 基于联合检测器的路面破损检测方法 ………………………………… 42
3.1.1 路面破损图像采集 ……………………………………………… 43
3.1.2 图像预处理 ……………………………………………………… 43
3.1.3 基于灰度分析的路面破损检测 ………………………………… 46
3.2 路面图像破损区域定位 ………………………………………………… 52
3.3 基于 Contourlet 变换的路面图像特征提取方法 ……………………… 53
3.3.1 Contourlet 变换 ………………………………………………… 54
3.3.2 其他纹理特征提取方法 ………………………………………… 56
3.4 支持向量机分类器 ……………………………………………………… 59
3.5 实验分析 ………………………………………………………………… 62
3.6 小结 ……………………………………………………………………… 64

下篇 驾驶人疲劳及异常行为信息感知

Chapter 4 Introduction of Driver's Fatigue and Abnormal Activities Detection …… 69

4.1 Introduction of driver's fatigue detection ……………………………… 69
4.2 Introduction of driver's abnormal activities detection ………………… 71

Chapter 5 Perception of Driver's Fatigue Information ……………………… 73

5.1 SEU fatigue expression data acquisition ……………………………… 73
5.2 Curvelet transform for image feature description …………………… 74
5.3 Support Vector Machines (SVMs) ……………………………………… 76
5.4 Other classification methods compared ……………………………… 80
5.5 Experiments ……………………………………………………………… 81

5.6　Conclusions ······ 86

Chapter 6　Perception of Driver's Abnormal Activities Information ······ 87
6.1　Data acquisition and features extraction of driving postures ······ 87
6.2　Features extraction by Nonsubsampled Contourlet Transform (NSCT) ······ 89
6.3　k-Nearest Neighbor (kNN) classifier ······ 91
6.4　Other classification methods compared ······ 92
6.5　Experimental results ······ 94
6.6　Conclusions ······ 98

参考文献 ······ 99

上 篇

车辆及路面信息感知

第一章
国内外的发展及研究现状

随着国民经济的快速增长,我国的道路交通运输事业在国民经济和居民生活中的地位也开始逐步的提升,计算机图像处理技术、通信与网络传输技术及电子技术的发展使得交通的智能化及现代化管理和控制成为可能,通过建立交通智能管理和控制体系,综合管理及控制人、车和路等交通参与体,对于提高交通运输效率和效益,保证交通安全,促进可持续发展具有十分重要的作用,已经引起世界许多国家的广泛重视。

将车辆检测应用于交通流量监控及统计分析、车辆自主导航和驾驶辅助系统等方面,对于提高车辆驾驶的安全性,实时发布交通流量信息诱导交通等具有重要的作用。为有效地实现路面破损的智能化检测,许多研究机构及学者对路面破损的自动检测技术进行了积极的探索和实验,相继提出了利用超声波、激光和数字图像处理技术实现对路面破损的检测识别。而目前应用最广泛的是基于数字图像处理技术的路面破损检测,该技术的应用是通过采集路面图像,对图像进行处理检测,识别到路面破损并实现路面破损的自动检测和分类。该技术在缓解劳动力的同时,也排除了人的主观因素的干扰,能够快速准确地进行公路路况的评价,但其检测识别的结果很大程度上取决于图像处理算法的选择,因此研究合适的图像处理算法对实现高精度的路面破损检测及自动化的路面破损识别分类具有重要意义。

1.1 车辆信息感知的研究现状

已经广泛应用于车辆检测的设施设备有磁感线圈、超声波、红外线及监控相机等。基于视频图像的车辆检测及分析是计算机视觉应用的一个分支,它通过结合图像处理及模式识别技术实现目标的自动检测及分析。通过监控相机和电脑模拟人眼的功能实现人工智能,使得视频图像检测技术日益成为交通监控系统中最具优势和最有发展潜力的检测方法。基于视频图像的车辆检测技术通过监控相机获得实时交通视频信息,结合图像处理原理和模式识别方法对图像进行实时处理和分析,计算得到交通流量、占有率、平均车速、排队长度等交通参数,并对车辆逆行、慢速、超速和交通阻塞等交通行为进行分析,并自动统计以及记录相关数据。综合交通参数及交通事件等重要信息,可对交通状态进行估计和预测,及时发布诱导信息或通过交警进行调控,从而保障交通正常安全运行。

目前车辆识别的研究大多局限于将牌照作为车辆的唯一身份特征,对于两种不同品牌及型号的车辆具有相同牌照(即盗牌)的问题,车牌识别系统无法辨识真伪。车辆品牌和型号识别在通道控制系统(ACS)中尤为重要,如停车场、大楼和限制区域通过识别车型限制假牌车辆进入。车型识别在交通管理领域同样发挥重要作用,如自动收费系统对不同类型车辆进行自动计费等功能。基于视频图像的车辆品牌及型号识别技术作为ITS中的一个重要分支,在打击盗窃车辆、规范交通秩序、大型停车场管理、高速公路自动计费和交通流量统计等方面具有广阔的应用前景。车辆类型识别的目的是向交通管理指挥中心报告通过通道闸口的车辆的类型、牌号、载重等参数,统计车流量、自动记录及结算通行车辆的费用等。由于视频图像中包含的信息内容丰富,因此,基于视频图像而进行的车型识别技术相较于其他监测技术而言更具有应用优势。通过视频图像手段提取到车辆前脸信息(包括车标、车牌、车灯及栅栏等信息),使用相应特征提取方法如多小波变换得到车辆前脸特征,与人脸识别类似,车辆前脸可以作为车辆的识别标准,该方法在监控套牌车辆应用中具有较大前景。

1.1.1 车辆区域检测方法研究现状

车辆区域检测及定位是车型分类的基础,国内外学者近年来相继提出了多种车辆检测方法,对于一幅在交通路口或路段相机获取的车辆图片,检测及定位车辆区域的难点在于区分路面、阴影、天空等背景及其他杂乱的噪声。Sun 等[1]将车辆分割方法分为基于先验知识的方法、基于立体的方法和基于运动的方法三类,其中第一种方法只需要单幅图片,后两种方法需要多幅图片或视频序列。如果对多幅图片和视频进行分析,可以使用背景差法[2,3]进行车辆检测,虽然背景差法比较方便,但它对光照条件,摄像机颤动及阴影等问题非常敏感,如果有少许的光照或相机位置的变动就要重新获取背景。

目前使用图像先验特征进行车辆检测的研究有很多,国内外研究机构和学者相继开展了车辆检测方法的研究,车辆的先验特征包括对称、颜色、阴影、几何(如角点、边缘)、纹理及车灯等特征,如 Gao 等[4]根据车尾灯为红色特点寻找车尾部红色区域并通过检测红色尾灯的对称轴定位车辆,其检测结果表明该方法在定位夜间车辆位置时效果显著;Guo 等[5]通过提取车辆周围物体颜色特征构建颜色模型以排除不真实或偏斜颜色;Techawatcharapaikul 等[6]使用颗边缘密度区分运动车辆区域及其阴影区域,该方法能有效检测简单交通场景中车辆并进行阴影区域提取,但当交通场景复杂和车辆及其阴影区域较小时错误率较高;Johansson 等[7]使用颜色圆柱体将车辆图像前景分为阴影和高亮区域,该方法能够在光照强度足够时进行车辆检测和追踪;Cucchiaral 等[8]通过检测夜间车辆车头灯定位车辆区域,但该方法易受地面反射物或车本身反射的影响。综上所述,车辆颜色、阴影及车灯特征对光照及背景变化比较敏感,存在阴雨天没有阴影、光照较强时颜色特征不明显及车灯主要用于夜间车辆检测等问题。

车辆区域特征提取及识别提供了一种有效的车辆检测方法。Kim[11]提取车辆图像灰度共生矩阵特征并使用支持向量机进行(SVM)车辆区域验证,根据 Kim 的分析,使用图像灰度共生矩阵(GLCM)作为纹理特征准确度较高;Kalinke 等[12]使用图像熵特征,图像熵特征能够有效描述感兴趣区域(ROI)内纹理特征,但检测精确度不如图像灰度共生矩阵特征;Wu[13]提取车辆区域小波变换特征并使用主成分分析(PCA)进行车辆识别;Sun[14]使用

Gabor 变换提取图像 Gabor 特征并且使用 SVM 分类器与神经网络分类器进行分类, Sun[14] 的实验结果显示使用 Gabor 特征及 SVM 识别效果较好。

关于车辆对称特征的研究,Zielke 等[15] 提出了使用基于图像亮度对称的车辆中心线的检测方法,该方法能够从背景中分割出车辆区域,但存在图像亮度对光照变化敏感的问题;Du 等[16] 提出使用车辆轮廓对称特征检测对称轴,令扫描线上每对像素"投票选取"对称轴,最后将得票最高的位置作为车辆对称轴,但由于该方法是对整幅图像进行计算,对称轴检测易受交通标志及道路边缘影响;Bin 等[17] 使用对称算子同时检测车辆竖直对称轴及车辆竖直边缘,该方法需要计算不同子窗口对称轴以满足车辆定位要求,这种方法时间复杂度过高;Teoh[18] 提出了通过计算不同窗口中水平扫描线上的对称值,并对对称值进行聚类分析以消除道路标志及建筑物的影响的方法,但这种方法对存在竖直对称特征的较大尺寸物体(如交通标志牌)比较敏感。

不仅限于车辆区域检测,在目标识别研究领域,Viola 和 Jones[19] 提出了使用 Haar 特征结合 Adaboost 分类器进行人脸检测,他们提出使用积分图像快速计算 Haar 特征,极大地提高了训练速度和检测效率,并提出了分类器的级联方式以提高检测速度;Dalal[20] 提出了使用 HOG 特征进行行人检测,研究表明,HOG 特征在特征描述方面具有卓越的性能,能够刻画目标局部边缘细节信息,使之能够推广到多种目标检测的应用;Chun-Hao Chang[21] 将 HOG 特征与 Gentle Adaboost 结合用于多视角车辆检测并获得了较好的检测效率及检测速度。

鉴于车辆对称轴易受路面上其他类对称物体如树木,路面标线等的影响,本文提出了一种基于车辆轮廓对称特征和车牌对称特征的特征融合方法,该方法首先检测车辆轮廓竖直对称轴,以车辆竖直对称轴为基准检测车牌水平和竖直对称轴,然后根据车牌对称轴定位车辆,这种方法能够有效消除噪声对车辆轮廓竖直对称轴检测的影响。同时,本文通过实验对比分析了基于边缘、车牌定位、纹理特征及 Gabor 特征等车辆检测方法的检测效率和时间复杂度。

1.1.2 车辆品牌及型号识别研究现状

目前有很多基于计算机视觉的车辆分类的研究,但是这些分类技术仅仅局限于区分不同类型的车辆,如小汽车、公交车和卡车等。近年来,有效识别车辆信息需求的增加,使得对识别车辆品牌和型号的技术研究显得日益迫切。目前商业上的车辆识别主要是对车牌进行识别,但根据警察和媒体的报告称,目前道路上存在的很多假牌及套牌车辆严重影响了公共安全。对车型进行识别可以提升通道控制系统(ACS)的可靠性,例如将自动车牌号码识别和车辆品牌及型号识别相结合,自动识别车辆的视觉信息(包括车辆品牌、型号和颜色信息等)。

车辆品牌及型号识别是一项比较新的技术。该技术的基本思路是提取车辆图像的合适特征,之后根据车辆特征进行车辆品牌和型号的识别。许多关于车辆分类的研究是基于车辆结构 3D 可变模板的车辆笼统分类(将车辆分为小汽车、公交车和大卡车等),Ferryman[22] 使用主成分分析(PCA)描述人工抽样几何数据表征车辆 3D 结构可变模板。将该模板与车辆图像进行匹配恢复车辆位置及结构后可进行不同类型车辆分类。Wei 等[23]对可变模板匹配进行了更深入的研究,他们使用多层神经网络实现基于模板的车辆分类。

  目前与车辆品牌及型号识别直接相关的论文还比较少。Petrivic[24,25]提出了一种根据图像梯度特征的车辆识别技术,包括引入直接梯度描述及统计映射等多种特征描述方法来描述车前脸感兴趣区域(ROI)特征,获得车前脸特征后使用最近距离分类法进行车辆识别。Munroe 和 Madden[26]采用机器学习分类技术进行车辆品牌和型号识别,首先使用腐蚀操作及 Canny 边缘检测算子提取特征向量,之后使用不同的机器学习分类器进行车辆品牌和型号的识别。Dlagnekov[27]和 Zafar 等[28]使用尺度不变特征变换(SIFT)[29]研究车辆品牌和型号识别问题,首先识别车辆图像中感兴趣点之后进行图像匹配。Zafar 等[28]通过将 SIFT 关键点检测限制于查询图像并选取具有最大似然估计面积的候选图像点的尺度不变特征转换(SIFT)描述子进行匹配。作为对 Dlagnekov[27]工作的延伸,Anthony[30]用能够表征轮廓线的特征代替尺度不变特征转换(SIFT)特征,首先提取车辆后部图像边缘,然后通过使用条形直线检测算法将边缘延展至直线段,最后进行图像匹配以实现车辆识别。Zafar 等[31]提出了使用二维线性统计判别分析(2DLDA)[32]进行车辆品牌和型号识别,2DLDA 可以最大化不同类之间的分散度与同类之间分散度的比例,这种方法显著优于之前提出的基于主成分分析(PCA)的方法。Kazemi 等[33]对比分析了快速傅里叶变换(FFT)特征、离散小波变换特征(DWT)和离散 Curvelet 变换特征进行车辆识别。Rahti 等[34]以图像 Contourlet 变换特征替换 Curvelet 变换进行车辆识别,作为对 Rahti[34]方法的延伸,Zafar[35]将限定子带内 Contourlet 特征作为车辆特征进行识别。Negri[36]使用面向轮廓点的选举算法进行不同种类车辆识别,这种方法在交通拥堵情况下尤为有效。Zhang[37]将 PHOG 特征和 Gabor 变换用于车辆特征描述,并使用随机森林(Random Forest)及旋转森林(Rotation Forest)进行分类器集成,同时赋予分类器"拒识"功能,提高了分类可靠性。

  国内相关研究人员也进行了车型识别技术的研究,如将车辆按尺寸及外形进行分类,杨文强[38]和季晨光[39]通过对车辆进行边缘提取获取车辆外形几何特征以此来进行车辆分类。也有学者主要专注于对车前脸每个部分特征提取的研究,如王枚[40]首先分割出车灯区域,然后使用图像的不变矩距离分类器在车标确定的车系中进行车灯识别。姚源[41]将车前脸分割成大灯、散热器栅栏等区域,并分别描述其形状特征,车辆前脸外形特征可以作为车型识别的基础。马蓓[42]提取了车前脸图像灰度共生矩阵特征(GLCM)并使用最小距离分类器进行车型识别。何得平[43]和赵英男[44]通过将车辆进行 Gabor 滤波获取车辆 Gabor 特征识别车型大小。

  纵观目前关于车辆品牌及型号识别的研究发展进度,设计出能够有效及实时识别车型的系统仍是一项富于挑战性的工作。车型识别问题可被当作一个多值分类问题来处理,在模式分类中又有两个重要问题需要解决,即特征描述和分类器设计。一个合适的车辆特征描述子应当能够区分不同品牌及型号的特点。几年来,计算机视觉的发展为我们提供了许多现成的特征描述子来处理图像分析问题。在众多的特征描述方法中,我们选择了使用已经成熟应用于行人检测的 HOG 特征[20],它通过计算每个小区间的梯度方向和幅值,并在更大的区间上进行梯度直方图归一化,最后将所有区间的梯度直方图串联起来得到特征向量。Contourlet 特征[34,45]作为第一代小波变换特征的延伸,能够对图像进行多尺度多方向的解读,是另外一种被广泛应用于图像识别的特征。

有了合适的图像特征描述子,车型识别系统可以通过使用分类算法完成。机器学习提供了大量先进的模式识别算法,包括支持向量机(SVM)[46]、神经网络[47]、集成分类器[48,49]及随机森林[50]等。集成分类器可以包含多个基分类器,如决策树和多层神经网络(MLP),即使用相同的多个基分类器处理输入样本。对于输入样本,集成分类器中每个基分类独立地对其进行识别,最后根据所有基分类器的结果进行综合判断,如使用多数投票表决的方法决定测试样本的最终类型。集成分类器的代表有 Bagging[48],AdaBoost[48]和随机子空间[51]等。最近,有一种基于主成分分析(PCA)被称为旋转森林的分类器集成方法,它能够在提升基分类器多样性的同时保证系统的精确度,该方法首先对随机分割的特征子集进行 PCA 分析,并使用每个特征子集的 PCA 系数构建旋转矩阵,实验证明这种方法比其他几种分类器集成的方法效果要好。

车型识别的精确度是学者们普遍追求的目标,他们致力于提出降低误识率的方法。但是在很多场景中例如监控场景,引入带有"拒识"选项的分类器来提高系统的可靠性显得更为重要,即放弃对某些不确定类型的样本识别。例如,警方需要鉴别某一时间点的盗牌车辆,当误识的代价比较高时,自动识别系统拒绝对置信度不高的样本识别并将这些样本留给人工进行详细的处理。可靠的识别系统允许特定领域知识和专家对分类器决策时施加额外的压力以控制精确度。尽管具有"拒识"选项的分类器近几年来一直是模式识别中研究的热点[52],并且已经有一些模型被提出来了[53],但提升系统识别的可靠性依然是研究的难点。

因此,本文的研究目标是提出具有"拒识"功能的分类器来提升系统的可靠性。在车型识别中如果对某测试样本的分类置信度超过某一提前设置的阈值,则接受对其的识别,如果置信度小于阈值则将该样本留给人工进行识别。换句话说,拒绝识别的目的就是通过将比较难识别的样本留给人工识别来提升系统的可靠性。设计分类识别系统的目的就是通过计算机帮助人类解决纷繁复杂的识别问题,我们不希望将过多的样本留给人工进行识别,因此,在保证系统可靠性的同时应提升系统对样本的正确识别率。类似于参考文献[37,54]中的方法,在本文中,我们设计一种级联集成分类器,在识别过程中,样本首先由级联的第一级集成分类器进行识别,此后将被第一级拒绝识别的样本送入第二级进行分类,第二级的集成分类器应具有更高的识别能力来处理被第一级拒绝掉的样本。相关的实验和理论会证明我们设计的具有"拒识"功能的级联集成分类器方法能够在保证系统可靠性的同时获得较高的正确识别率。根据文献综述介绍的关于车辆检测及车型分类关键技术难点及研究现状,本文提出了新的车辆检测方法并设计了一种可靠性较高的车型识别方案。

1.2 公路路面信息感知的研究现状

公路特别是高等级公路已成为衡量一个国家经济水平和现代化程度的标志之一,其建设、管理和运营也极大地促进了我国经济的发展。与此同时,随着社会的进步,居民生活水平的提高,汽车保有量也开始大幅度的提升,受交通量的增加以及车辆大型化、超载严重等现象的影响,使得高等级公路在使用过程中经受严重的考验,导致路面破损的出现,严重影响道路交通的安全性和舒适性。因此,实施公路养护工作是公路管理部门的工作重点。目前,我国高速公路呈现出建设和养护双高峰重合的特点。高速公路的年养护量(大、中修工程)在8 000公里以上。对于公路养护管理者来说,面临的养护任务越来越重,压力越来越大,如何搞好高速公路的养护管理工作已是一个不可回避的现实问题。

路面养护是公路养护的重点,其质量的好坏直接影响道路交通的安全性和舒适性,而路面破损状况作为路面养护管理工作的依据在路面养护决策中占据重要地位。传统的路面破损检测方法是采用人工检测,但该方法工作效率低,劳动强度大,作业危险程度较高,对裂缝的检测判别凭借检测人员的主观经验判断,存在较高的主观性,且受天气条件等影响较为严重,已不能适应高等级公路快速发展的需求。因此研究设计智能化的路面破损检测方法成为提高路面养护管理工作的关键热点问题之一。直观上,路面破损图像往往具有以下显著特点:①路面破损位置的灰度较破损位置周围正常路面的灰度要暗;②路面破损处会出现灰度梯度跳变;③路面破损具有局部连通性。基于路面破损图像的上述三个特性,国内外研究机构和学者相继开展了一系列路面破损检测方法的研究。

1.2.1　路面图像预处理技术现状

由于采集的路面图像受路面材料和路面环境的影响,往往存在砂砾、碎石、杂物等噪声的影响,且受光照影响较大,因此在对路面图像进行检测工作之前,均要对路面图像进行预处理及图像增强,以达到消除路面图像噪声,强化路面破损的效果,为路面破损检测提供基础。Jitprasithsiri和Sun提出了采用非线性滤波的方法对图像进行增强处理[55,56],前者利用中值滤波算法对路面破损图像进行增强,在去除一定噪声的同时保证了图像中裂缝目标的边缘不会失真,后者考虑到存在噪声的图像裂缝与背景之间的低对比度,利用原始图像与高斯低通滤波图像作差分运算实现图像去噪处理。孙波成等[57]提出了空域滤波以及掩膜平滑法等图像增强方法,其所利用的空域滤波是通过小区域模板卷积的方法,实现将模板中心和图像中待处理的某像素点重合,并将模板各元素与模板下各自的对应像素值相乘,最后将模板输出响应作为当前模板中心所在像素的灰度值。为了更好地突出图像线形特征的方向性,通常的做法是对上述单模板进行扩展,构造8个方向的模板实现对图像的增强。Koutsopoulos等[58]利用差影法,对于路面破损图像,将其与不含破损的路面图像做差分,则使得图像中的破损信息突显出来,实现了破损图像中目标的增强。

上述几种方法只有当路面破损图像内容较简单时,才能取得较好的效果。但一般情况下路面破损图像较为复杂,因此基于模糊、数学形态学和信息量等人工智能技术的路面病害图像增强方法,得到许多研究人员的关注。Chou[59]、Cheng[60]和Li等[61]提出了基于模糊理论的图像增强方法,在传统模糊理论的基础上对其加以改进并提出了最大模糊熵阈值、模糊掩盖处理以及灰度熵模糊法等方法。郭宝良[62]和欧阳琰[63]也通过对传统模糊理论的模糊隶属度函数进行了改进处理,实现图像增强的效果,但模糊增强方法的缺点是容易在模糊背景的同时对路面破损也有一定程度的削弱,不利于对检测后期目标特征的提取。Cheng等[64]根据路面图像的灰度特征,提出了针对路面破损图像的增强算法,其处理的路面破损图像包括三类像素,一种是低频、宽幅值信号,代表的是亮度不均匀的背景像素,一种是宽幅值且边缘具有高频分量的幅值信号,代表图像中的破损目标,以及高频窄幅信号代表的噪声像素,并根据三类像素信号频谱的不同对图像中破损目标像素进行增强处理,算法取得了较好的效果。Nejad 等[65]利用直方图均衡化和快速傅里叶变换对图像进行增强处理,其快速傅里叶变换是针对图像的像素块(32×32)进行的傅里叶变换,但使用该方法处理后的图像有一定的边际效应。陈利利[12]提出了一种基于多尺度图像分析的路面病害研究方法,其基于多尺度分析,从形态学多尺度分析和非线性扩散多尺度分析两个方面对路面图像进行平滑处理,并基于形态学的各向异性扩散方程,利用形态学算子简化图像数据,保存必要的形状特征以及消除不相关性的特点,对图像进行形态学多尺度去噪处理,该方法能较好地保持图像边缘和细节,抑制边界移动,同时能有效地去除噪声。类似于小波变换去噪,许多学者通过将图像转换至频率域对图像频谱进行频域变换以实现图像增强,Wang 等[67]和 Wu 等[68]提出了一种利用 Shearlet 变换对图像进行去噪的处理方法,该方法采用低频率部分的背景匹配和在多层阈值分割下对高频率部分的大尺度 Shearlet 变换,实现图像中噪声信息的去除。李刚[69]和胡士昆等[70]提出了一种基于 Contourlet 变换的图像增强去噪方法,该方法采用基于完全冗余的 Contourlet 变换、基于数学形态学的 Contourlet 变换和非下采样轮廓变换(NSCT)对路面裂缝图像实现增强。吕岩[71]提出了一种基于 Beamlet 变换的裂缝图像匀光算法。董立文等[72]提出了一种利用小波系数尺度间相关性的局部自适应去噪方法来实现路面破损图像增强,针对小波系数估计中硬阈值方法和软阈值方法的缺点,通过对双重量收缩函数得到的阈值乘以一个合适系数进行修订的折中。

综上所述,各研究机构和学者提出的方法都通过实验得到验证,但是,由于实验数据格式不同,这些图像增强技术在具体实践中往往存在偏差。本文所研究的路面图像数据是由高分辨率线阵 CCD 相机采集,能够实现毫米级裂缝的图像采集,但易受光照和道路环境影响,采集的路面图像中存在阴影且亮度较低,因此,本文在上述研究成果的基础上,对线阵 CCD 图像增强技术进行研究,以增强路面病害图像的高可靠性。

1.2.2 路面破损检测技术研究现状

路面破损检测是路面破损识别的基础,近些年来,国内外学者在路面破损检测技术方面做出了大量的研究探索。Huang 等[73]提出了一种利用直方图分析检测路面破损的方法。假设含有裂缝区域的路面破损图像的灰度直方图具有双峰特性,并据此确定一个阈值对路面破损图像进行分割,该方法对路面破损明显的图像较为有效,裂缝与路面背景对比度较低时该方法的检测效果较差。Li 等[74]提出了一种利用 Sobel 边缘检测路面破损的方法。其假定路面噪声区域的像素点周长小于 20 像素,而路面破损区域的像素点周长大于 20 像素,从而根据周长的大小实现噪声信息的去除,并得到路面破损图像分割结果,该方法的缺点是当图像中破损信息较为丰富复杂时,采用硬阈值判断容易导致破损的误判,影响后续对裂缝的识别分类。Grivas 等[75]提出了一种利用区域生长技术对路面破损图像进行分割处理的方法。Yan 等[76]探讨了利用数学形态学进行路面破损识别的可行性。

在分析路面破损图像几何相关性的基础上,冯永安[77]、李莉[78]和李晋惠等[79]提出了对 Sobel 算子模板进行改进后的 8 方向的 Sobel 算子模板,该方法利用图像边缘附近的亮度阈变这一特性,把在邻域内灰度变化超过某个适当阈值的像素点当做边缘点,以此来检测路面破损,但利用该方法检测到的路面破损边缘较粗,有时会产生伪边缘,且对噪声的影响较为敏感。唐磊等[80]通过对路面裂缝构建三维曲面模型,将裂缝视为模型中的山谷,通过三维曲率的计算检测到"山谷"位置及裂缝位置来实现对裂缝的检测,该方法存在的缺陷是由于算法的局限性导致检测到的裂缝往往出现断裂的现象,且需要结合其他算法使用。2003年,Huo 等[81]提出了一种对细小特征运用复杂图表进行多尺度检测的方法,该方法利用 Beamlets 对线性分段进行并行组织的多尺度系统,建立与 Beamlet 分析相关的算法以从含噪声图像中复原线性片段。

利用数学统计学的新进展,形成了从噪声图像中提取细小片段或细小特征的多尺度方法来对路面破损进行检测。Kumar 等[82]采用 Gabor 滤波及其变形来检测路面图像纹理破损。张雷等[83]利用 Hear 变换对路面破损图像进行低通滤波处理,并对图像进行分块处理及自适应阈值以实现路面破损区域的自动分割。李刚等[84]基于大津法对路面破损图像进行分割,并依据轮廓跟踪原理计算出路面破损区域的面积、周长等参数,并利用互信息量求取最优阈值,从而对路面破损区域提取特征。赵吉广[85]针对路面破损图像,对比研究了全局阈值与动态阈值相结合的最大类间方差法和基于直方图阈值分割的阈值插值算法。Zhang[86]提出了一种将人工生命系统理论应用于路面病害检测的方法,该方法通过使用不同结构的人造生物结构对图像进行卷积处理,以实现对裂缝的检测,该方法对路面上油污黑点等有很好的去除作用,但算法结构较为复杂,不适用于对大量图像的检测。

综上所述,这些路面破损检测方法的主要局限性在于方法的普适性不高,针对各种不同路面破损的检测精度不高。本文针对线阵 CCD 路面破损图像,研究高精度的路面破损检测方法。

1.2.3 路面破损分类技术研究现状

路面破损区域目标分类前提是对路面破损目标的特征描述,常用的特征描述子有灰度特征、纹理特征和几何形状特征等,目前,对于路面破损图像的特征描述,使用较多的是采用区域及几何特征描述子,路面图像的区域特征包括傅立叶变换特征和矩描述特征等。对此,国内外研究学者提出了诸多特征描述方法,如:Haralick 等[87]提出了一种利用统计学的路面破损图像特征提取方法,该方法利用灰度级协方差矩阵或灰度的自相关性对裂缝信息进行特征提取。Paquis 等[88]从结构学的角度出发,提出了一种基于多分辨率协方差矩阵的形态学金字塔变换的特征提取方法。Jain 等[89]和 Mallat 等[90]分别提出了基于 Gabor 变换和快速傅里叶变换的路面图像破损特征提取方法。欧阳琰[63]提出了一种基于几何距离可分性的特征提取方法。肖旺新[91]提出了一种基于破损密度因子的路面破损特征提取方法,并利用该方法对路面破损图像进行了分类实验。储江伟等[92]利用原始灰度值的直方图特征作为子块路面图像特征,并进行了实验研究。

路面破损类型的自动识别是实现智能化路面破损检测系统的关键技术之一,国内外学者相继开展了探索研究。Wang 等[93]在对图像进行背景光照均衡化后,对图像进行 Shearlet 变换去噪处理,然后利用 Radon 变换对图像进行分类。Radon 变换是利用不同角度的裂缝所对应形成的 Radon 变换方向与位置的不同这一特点对路面裂缝进行分类,该方法的缺点是只适用于裂缝类病害,对于坑槽等形状不规则的路面破损类型则不适用。Nejad 等[65]提出了一种基于 Wavelet-Radon 变换和动态神经网络(DNN)的路面病害检测和分类方法,该方法通过 Wavelet-Radon 变换对路面破损进行分割特征提取,再利用 DNN 实现对路面破损的分类。欧阳琰[63]提出了一种基于聚类分析的路面破损分类方法,该方法采用C-均值聚类算法实现对路面破损的识别分类。李刚[84]提出的方法基于裂缝的投影性质,依据投影量的大小和方向初步判定路面破损的程度和类型,再对线性裂缝与不规则网状裂缝进行初步区分,并利用欧拉数(即图像目标连接体数与其中的孔洞数之差)的大小对裂缝进行分类处理。该方法仅对裂缝类病害进行分类,且仅适用于对单个目标的分类。孙奥[94]提出了一种利用支持向量机对路面病害进行分类的方法。

综上所述,这些方法的局限主要有:各种算法往往只适用于裂缝类病害,而对于非裂缝类不规则破损分类效果较弱;各类方法在分类实验时采用的数据样本数量都比较小。在上述研究成果的基础上,本文针对 CCD 路面破损图像,研究高效率的路面破损图像特征提取及分类方法。

第二章
车辆信息感知理论与技术

本章主要研究内容为：首先提出一种新的车辆区域检测方法，确定车型识别感兴趣区域（ROI），之后提取感兴趣区域（ROI）图像特征，最后引入一种带有"拒识"功能的级联集成分类器对车辆图像特征进行识别。

首先，分析车辆图像数据来源、筛选及预处理方法。对于一幅输入的监控图像，研究定位车辆所在位置的方法。分析车辆几何、颜色及纹理特征，进而在现有检测方法的基础上改进车辆检测方法。根据车辆区域假设和验证步骤研究两类方法进行车辆区域检测：第一类是直接使用车辆先验知识，即车牌、车辆边缘和车辆对称特征进行检测；第二类是提取车辆特征并使用分类器进行车辆区域识别。通过分别研究基于车辆边缘、车牌、车辆对称特征、车辆纹理特征及车辆图像 Gabor 特征 5 种检测算法的检测效率和计算复杂度，分析得出适于智能交通车辆监控、车型识别及车辆分类的车辆区域定位方法。根据车辆区域包围框定位出能够表征车辆品牌和型号的区域，即车前脸区域。

其次，研究图像特征描述方法。首先研究基于特征融合的车辆图像特征描述方法，分别提取图像梯度方向直方图（HOG）和 Contourlet 特征，使用不同特征融合的方法描述车前脸特征，通过实验比较得出能够有效表征车前脸独特性的特征描述方法。其次，研究特征降维及特征融合方法，直接使用特征描述子所提取的特征维数都比较高，并且分类器的训练会占用大量时间。因此本文研究使用了主成分分析法（PCA）对特征线性变换而达到提取主要维度的目的。另外，在第三章探讨了特征融合的相关研究进展，并提出将两种特征简单串联成一种新的车辆特征描述子，并在实验阶段验证了该种方法的有效性。

最后，研究具有"拒识"功能的级联集成分类器，级联分类器的第一级集成分类器由不同的基分类器组成，选用的四种基分类器包括朴素贝叶斯，k-近邻（kNN），支持向量机（SVM），多层神经网络（MLP），分别使用 HOG 和 Contourlet 变换特征作为输入特征进行训练，对比每种特征及分类器结合的识别效率，同时建立基于多数表决分类机制的集成分类器，拒绝识别没有达到多数表决阈值的输入特征，并将该特征对应的模糊图像送入第二级级联分类器进行识别；第二级集成分类器是基于神经网络的旋转森林集成分类器，基分类器使用相同的 MLP 网络，对被第一级拒绝识别的样本进行识别，第二级分类器也带有"拒识"功能，我们通过设计两级分类器级联将被拒绝识别的样本降低到一个可以被人工处理接受的水平，同时又保证了系统的可靠性。

2.1 车辆图像采集及车辆目标区域检测

进行模式识别需要大量的实验数据作为支撑,本章介绍本文所使用图像数据来源及筛选过程。同时,由于车辆类型识别是根据感兴趣区域(ROI)特征结合分类器实现的,车辆前脸(包括散热器,车标及车灯等)特征能够有效描述一辆车的类型信息,因此,我们首先研究了一种车辆区域定位方法,之后根据车牌位置和车辆前脸尺寸关系定位出感兴趣区域(ROI)。为了完成本文所涉及相关图像处理和模式识别相关算法的实验验证,我们需要准备一些车辆图像数据。苏州交通局独墅湖高教区分局为我们的科学研究提供了原始的图像数据,这些数据是由交通监控相机记录一个月所产生。图像由安装在10个交叉口的CCD相机在每天8:00~18:00的时间段内触发获取,包含不同的天气及光照情况。从这些大量的图像数据中(每天数据>20 000),我们选取了包含15种品牌的18种车型共4 500张图片,这些车型包括奥迪(Audi),别克(Buick)(2种),长安(Changan),奇瑞(Chery)(2种),雪佛兰(Chevrolet),雪铁龙(Citroen),福特(Ford),本田(Honda),现代(Hyundai)(2种),马自达(Mazda),日产(Nissan),标志(Peugeot),大众(Volkswagen),丰田(Toyota)和五菱(Wulin)。其中,有些车型是同一品牌的不同类型,如现代索纳塔(SONATA)和现代伊兰特(ELANTRA),这两种车型的外观有很大不同。如果一些品牌的不同车型具有类似的外观,如 Audi A7 和 Audi A8,别克凯越(Excelle)和别克Xt,我们将他们归为一种车型。所有图像数据均包含一辆正面车辆影像,车辆到摄像头的距离远近不一。原始图像的大小为1 024×1 360,如图2-1所示为一部分图像数据。

图2-1 部分图像数据

从图 2-1 中可得，大部分车辆外观不同，在车辆前部具有丰富的边缘信息。如图 2-2 所示，数据库中车辆图像具有很大的不同，主要表现在车辆位置、尺度、角度及光照等方面。

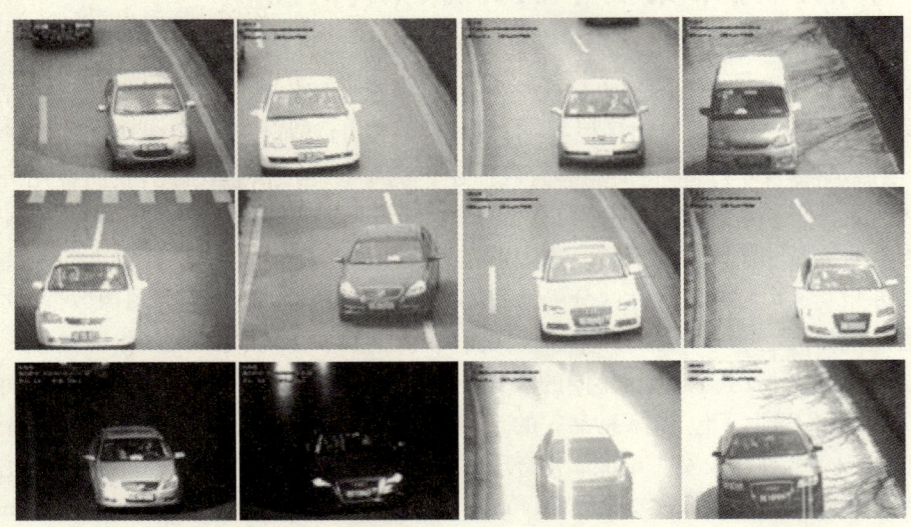

图 2-2　不同位置、角度、光照条件的车辆图像

在目标识别系统中有两个重要的问题需要解决，即目标区域检测和识别问题。在车型识别系统中，车辆区域的检测和定位尤其重要，这是由于车型识别是基于车辆感兴趣区域（即前脸区域）进行的，因此本文首先研究一种车辆区域检测方法，并结合车辆区域和车牌位置定位出车辆前脸区域作为车型识别系统的输入图像。

2.1.1　基于对称特征的车辆检测方法

以车辆轮廓竖直对称轴作为定位车辆区域是一种有效的检测方法，但车辆轮廓对称轴易受树木、道路标线等噪声的影响。本文根据车辆轮廓存在竖直对称轴和车牌存在水平和竖直对称轴的特点，首先检测车辆轮廓竖直对称轴，以车辆轮廓对称轴位置为参考检测车牌水平和竖直对称轴，最后根据所检测到的车牌水平和竖直对称轴进行车辆区域及车型识别感兴趣区域（ROI）定位。首先生成输入灰度图像的边缘图像，采用拉普拉斯算子进行车辆边缘检测，之后对边缘图像进行中值滤波，中值滤波结果在消除噪声的同时保存了图像中的细节部分。拉普拉斯（Laplace）算子是不依赖于边缘方向的二阶微分算子，对于数字图像，拉普拉斯变换可以借用模板实现，模板函数可以表示为

$$G(i,j) = |4f(i,j) - f(i+1,j) - f(i-1,j) - f(i,j+1) - f(i,j-1)|$$

(2-1)

其中，$G(i,j)$ 为将 (i,j) 处的像素值 $f(i,j)$ 使用 Laplace 算子计算后的结果，图 2-3 为输入图像灰度化后使用 Laplace 算子进行边缘检测及滤波后的结果。

(a) 输入图像　　　　　　　　　　　　(b) 边缘检测

图 2-3　输入图像及车辆边缘检测结果

考虑到车辆区域在监控图像固定范围内，为减少运算量，图像边缘区域可以不作考虑，设置车辆对称轴搜索区域如图 2-4(a)所示，计算水平扫描线上每个像素点的对称值[18]：

$$V(x,y) = \sum_{x'=1}^{W/2} S(x, x', y') \tag{2-2}$$

$$S(x, x', y') = \begin{cases} 5, & f(x-x', y') = f(x+x', y') = 255 \\ -1, & f(x-x', y') \neq f(x+x', y') \\ 0, & f(x-x', y') = f(x+x', y') = 0 \end{cases} \tag{2-3}$$

其中，$V(x,y)$ 为 (x,y) 处对称值，W 为计算每个像素点对称值的幅宽，本文根据车辆图像的像素宽度假设为 300，x' 为当前搜索水平扫面线上像素的横坐标，y' 为当前水平扫描线纵坐标，每条扫描线上像素对称值计算结果如图 2-4(b)所示。

 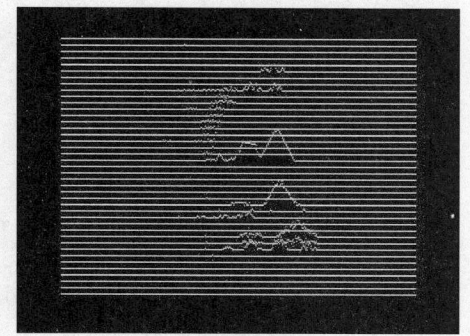

(a) 车辆对称轴搜索区域　　　　　　　　(b) 扫描线对称值计算

图 2-4　车辆轮廓对称轴搜索区域及搜索区域内水平扫面线对称值计算

根据车辆轮廓几何特征，车辆轮廓对称值在其竖直对称轴处最大而在车辆边缘处对称值最小，根据公式(2-4)计算每列对称值之和：

$$Vcol(x) = \sum_{n=0}^{M} V(x, n*val) \tag{2-4}$$

其中，val 为行距，$Vcol(x)$ 为第 x 列对称值之和。对 $Vcol(x)$ 进行排序，得到最大对称值 $Vcol(x_m)$ 对应列 x_m 作为车辆轮廓的对称轴。

对称轴上决定对称值大小的像素点集中在车辆边缘信息最丰富的区域，如散热器、车灯所在区域，以此可以搜索对称轴上最大对称值区段，使用以下公式检索对称值最大区段：

$$Vcol(x_m, n) = \sum_{n=i}^{i+5} V(x_m, n*val), \quad i = 1, 2, \cdots, M \tag{2-5}$$

得到 $Vcol(x_m, n)$ 最大时对应的扫描行 n_m，对应图像纵坐标为 $y_m = n_m * val$。图 2-5(a) 所示竖直线为实验车辆图像的对称轴，白色圆点 (x_m, y_m) 为对称值最大区段起始行，由计算结果可以看出对称轴上最大对称值区段所在行车辆轮廓信息最丰富。考虑到车辆轮廓丰富区域一般在车辆散热器和车灯等位置，本文以车辆轮廓对称轴上最大对称值区段起始行作为参考点，该参考点位于车牌上方且位置变化范围较大，若以该点作为车辆轮廓定位参考点则定位误差较大，可以此参考点为基准搜索车牌水平和竖直对称轴所在位置。

以参考点 (x_m, y_m) 作基准，在其下方搜索车牌水平和竖直对称轴。设参考点 (x_m, y_m) 到车辆轮廓对称轴搜索窗下边缘距离为 δ，车牌水平对称轴搜索区域为参考点到搜索下边缘距离 δ 的 β_1 到 β_2 倍，$\beta_1 = 0.2$，$\beta_2 = 0.8$，如图 2-5(b) 中竖直扫描线区域。计算车牌水平对称轴搜索区域每条竖直扫描线上像素点对称值，将每行对称值之和最大行作为车牌水平对称轴，图 2-5(b) 中水平线所示位置即车牌水平对称轴 y_s。

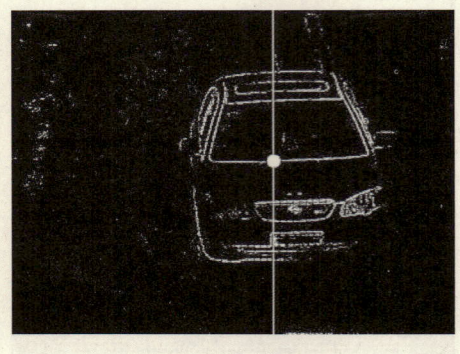 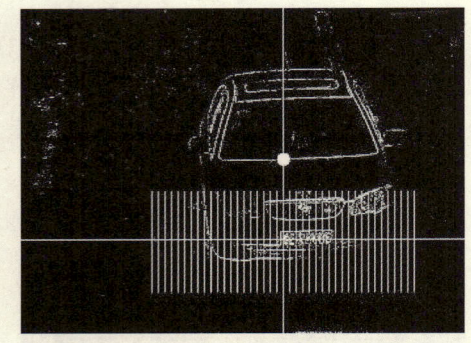

(a) 轮廓对称轴　　　　　　　　　　(b) 车牌对称轴确定

图 2-5　车辆轮廓对称轴及车牌对称轴搜索区域

在由点 $(x_m - \delta_1, y_s - \delta_2)$ 和 $(x_m + \delta_1, y_s + \delta_2)$ 确定的矩形范围内搜索车牌竖直对称轴，与车牌水平对称轴计算方法相同，计算车牌竖直对称轴，图 4(a) 中处于车辆轮廓对称轴右方的竖直线即为车牌竖直对称轴 x_s，车牌水平对称轴和竖直对称轴交点为 (x_s, y_s)。根据车辆对称轴和基准点假设车辆区域，假设车辆区域在由 $(x_s - w, y_s - h_t)$ 和 $(x_s + w, y_s + h_b)$ 确定的矩形包围框内。使用基于灰度积分投影的方法搜索车辆区域，边缘图像竖直及水平积分投影计算公式为

$$v_i = \sum_{j=1}^{2w} f(x_i, y_j) \tag{2-6}$$

$$h_i = \sum_{i=1}^{h_b+h_t} f(x_i, y_j) \qquad (2\text{-}7)$$

其中,$f(x, y)$ 是点 (x, y) 处的像素值,如图 2-6(a)所示为假设区域内车辆灰度水平和竖直投影直方图。

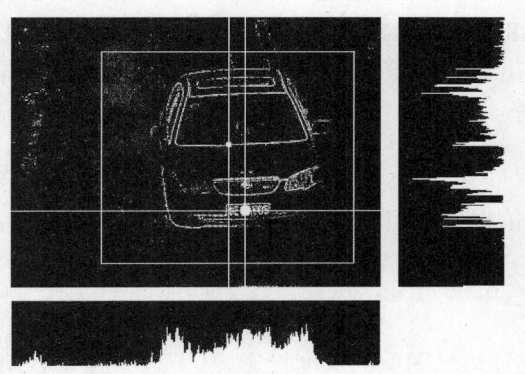

(a) 车辆区域假设　　　　　　　　(b) 车辆区域验证

图 2-6　车辆区域假设及车辆区域验证

分别计算竖直和水平积分投影的最大值 m_v 及 m_h,从上向下搜索水平投影目标像素个数超过阈值 $0.5m_h$ 的第一行作为上边界,从左到右搜索竖直投影目标像素个数超过阈值 $0.5m_v$ 的第一列作为左边界,使用同样的方法搜索得到右边界和下边界。图 2-6(b)为车辆区域检测的最终结果。

2.1.2　其他车辆检测方法

作为与车辆对称特征检测方法的比较,本文分别使用其他 4 种方法进行车辆区域检测:第一类是直接使用车辆先验知识,即车牌、车辆边缘进行检测;第二类是首先提取车辆纹理、Gabor 特征,之后使用支持向量机(SVM)进行训练学习后进行车辆检测。

1) 基于边缘的车辆区域检测方法

Song[95]通过检测车辆虚拟上视图(virtual top-view)竖直边缘定位车辆边缘,有效解决了远距离车辆边缘信息不足的问题。Ha[96]提出一种基于运动边缘检测的方法来区分车辆边缘及车辆阴影边缘,有效消除了车辆阴影边缘对运动车辆追踪的影响。本文所用车辆图像使用 Laplace 算子进行边缘检测,在消除噪声的同时保存了车辆边缘,可以直接进行车辆区域搜索,使用灰度投影统计的方法搜索车辆轮廓区水平和竖直边缘。

根据行车原理,车辆靠右行驶,超车车辆在其左道行驶,监控相机所获图片右下方噪声比较少,因此可首先确定车辆区域矩形框右下角点。从下向上搜索水平投影目标像素个数超过阈值 T 的第一行作为下边界 y_b,从右到左搜索竖直投影目标像素个数超过阈值 T 的第一列作为右边界 x_r,将右下角点 (x_r, y_b) 作为参考点,假设车辆区域在由 $(x_r - w, y_b - h)$、(x_r, y_b) 两点确定的矩形包围框内(其中 w, h 分别为假设车辆区域的宽带和长度），之后在预选框内使用同样方法搜索上边界和左边界。

2）基于车牌定位的车辆区域检测方法

Nikul[9]对图像进行形态学计算、YCbCr颜色空间分割及边缘检测方法定位车牌区域，该方法能够有效检测印度车辆车牌区域。Zheng[10]使用竖直Sobel算子检测车辆图像竖直边缘并排除过长或过短的竖直边缘以筛选出车牌区域，通过对中文车牌检测实验，表明该方法具有较好的鲁棒性。类似Zheng[10]提出的方法，本文根据车牌区域灰度投影变化比较剧烈的特点，使用图像列与列相减的方法突出车牌区域，同时噪声点在相减的过程中得到削弱，列相减即计算图像水平方向的一阶差分：

$$f(i,j) = f(i,j+1) - f(i,j) \tag{2-8}$$

图像列与列相减后，将图像进行阈值化，阈值根据列相减后自身灰度分布确定，阈值为：

$$T = \frac{1}{2m}\sum_{i=1}^{m}\max f(x_i, y) \tag{2-9}$$

其中，m为列数，$f(x,y)$为输入图像。统计边缘图像的灰度投影，从下往上搜索到第一行目标像素个数大于阈值T时作为车牌下边界y_b，根据车牌高度估计上边界y_t，之后在上下边界内使用同样方法搜索左边界x_l和右边界x_r。根据车牌颜色RGB三分量差别较大的特点，在输入彩色图像中验证估计车牌区域内颜色差异较大的区域作为车牌的最终区域。车牌尺寸与车辆尺寸存在一定的比例关系，可以根据车牌位置和尺寸估计车辆区域。

3）基于车辆纹理及支持向量机（SVM）的检测方法

将输入图像灰度化后网格化为$M \times N$个尺寸为$W \times H$的子图，将子图灰度级量化为16级，提取每个窗口图像灰度共生矩阵，其灰度共生矩阵为16×16维，以列优先将其重排为256维的支持向量机SVM[97,98]输入向量，选取车辆区域和背景区域样本子图像提取其纹理特征，使用支持向量机（SVM）进行训练。使用SVM训练结果对输入测试图像的每个子图像的灰度共生矩阵特征向量进行识别，判断每个矩形格是否属于车辆区域。由于相邻矩形格之间的灰度相关性，识别结果会产生一些噪声，通过计算所有被识别为车辆区域方格中心坐标的均值(x_{mean}, y_{mean})，遍历每个被识别为车辆区域方格中心坐标(x, y)，计算其与中心坐标均值(x_{mean}, y_{mean})的距离：

$$\delta = \sqrt{(x_i - x_{mean})^2 + (y_i - y_{mean})^2} \tag{2-10}$$

真实车辆窗口应为与中心距离小于某阈值T的区域，若某窗口与中心距离较大则为噪声。

4）基于Gabor特征及支持向量机（SVM）的检测方法

将输入车辆图像划分为$M \times N$个网格，用$m \times n$个网格表示车辆或背景区域，以行优先规则遍历每个$m \times n$窗口，计算每个$m \times n$窗口的Gabor响应特征，如取$M=N=8, m=3, n=4$，则每幅图片共有30个子窗口。将每个子窗口中图像分布与Gabor滤波器函数[99,100]计算卷积，得到每个窗口的Gabor响应，将Gabor响应的统计量均值、方差和偏态作为Gabor特征，假设使用3尺度、4方向滤波器组，将每个滤波器与图像卷积，则特征向量维数为$3 \times 4 \times 3 = 36$维。分别选取若干车辆区域和背景区域计算Gabor特征，将样本

Gabor 特征使用 SVM 进行训练,将每张测试图片的所有交叠窗口均作为假设车辆区域,使用 SVM 训练结果识别每张图片的 30 个子窗口,识别出车辆区域和背景区域。

2.1.3 感兴趣区域(ROI)定位

车辆引擎盖下方包含车标、车灯及散热器的前脸区域反映了车辆类型的主要信息,而不同类型车辆引擎盖上方的挡风玻璃部位则大同小异,因此车型分类的感兴趣区域(ROI)是车辆前脸区域。结合本章提出的对称轴检测方法及车牌检测方法定位车牌,首先定位到车牌对称中心,以对称中心假设车牌搜索区域,假设区域如图 2-7 所示。

图 2-7 车牌位置搜索

由于监控相机角度及位置固定,所拍摄图像中车牌尺寸固定,假设车牌大小为 $W \times H$,在车牌搜索区域内进行遍历匹配,统计每个大小为 $W \times H$ 窗口内的目标像素个数,当目标像素个数超过某一阈值时将对应窗口标记为车牌区域,否则排除该窗口,像素个数阈值满足以下要求

$$T = \rho \sum_i \sum_j f(i,j) \tag{2-11}$$

其中,$\sum_i \sum_j f(i,j)$ 为搜索区域内所有目标像素个数,ρ 为系数,决定阈值 T 的大小。搜索遍历的示意图如图 2-7 所示。考虑到车辆前脸图像尺寸与车牌图像尺寸之间的固定关系,假设车牌的宽度为 w_p,使用图 2-8(a)所示的方法确定车辆前脸感兴趣区域,图 2-8(b)是最终获取的车脸 ROI 区域。

(a) 车辆图像 ROI 区域检测　　　　(b) 车脸 ROI 区域

图 2-8 根据车牌位置确定感兴趣区域

作为车型识别及分类的基础,选取品牌分别为 Audi、Buick、Changan、Chery、Chevrolet、Citroen、Ford、Honda、Hyundai、Mazda、Nissan、Peugeot、Toyota、Volkswagen 及 Wulin 这 15 种不同品牌车辆实验图片,每种类型 30 张共 450 张由监控相机获取的车辆图片。

本文所述算法在 VC6.0 环境下开发,使用 OpenCV[66](开源计算机视觉库)实现图像处理操作,电脑配置为 Intel Core Duo2.0 GHz。分别使用基于边缘、基于车牌和基于车辆对称特征三种方法对 450 张实验图片进行检测,并与 Teoh[18] 提出的车辆轮廓对称轴检测方法进行比较,输入图片尺寸为 1 024×1 360,当车辆包围框覆盖车辆 90% 以上区域且包围框尺寸与车辆尺寸相差不超过 10% 时为正确识别。

随机选取 150 张图片作为基于 GLCM 特征和 SVM 车辆检测、基于 Gabor 特征和 SVM 车辆检测的训练图片,对于基于 GLCM 特征的检测,将图片网格化,提取每个子窗口的灰度共生矩阵,使用 SVM 对样本图片进行训练,之后用训练后的结果对数据库中其余 300 张图片进行识别;对于基于 Gabor 特征的检测,按 2.3.4 小节方法划分图像,则 150 张图片共划分为 1 500 张子图像,选取训练样本中车辆子图像作为车辆目标图像,另外选取 500 张背景子图像,使用 Gabor 滤波器组分别提取车辆和背景子图像的 Gabor 特征,本文 Gabor 滤波器组为 4 尺度、6 方向,则 Gabor 特征为 72 维,之后将样本特征使用 SVM 训练,使用训练结果检测其余 150 张图片。六种车辆检测方法的检测结果如表 2.1 所示。

表 2.1 六种车辆检测方法的检测率及检测时间

结果\方法	融合特征	轮廓特征	车牌	GLCM	Gabor	Teoh[18]
检测率	90.7%	82.8%	80.9%	86.4%	80.8%	87.6%
检测时间(ms)	125	140	125	6 513	17 609	109

实验结果表明本文所提出基于对称特征的车辆检测方法检测率为 90.7%,比 Teoh[18] 中基于轮廓对称特征的检测准确率高 3.1%,同时我们的方法在检测率和检测时间上优于其他的方法,如基于 GLCM、Gabor 特征和 SVM 进行分类的方法。从表 2.1 中可以看出,本文的方法在检测时间上是最短的,这对车辆实时检测和识别等应用具有重要意义。

在车型识别中,我们首先要根据车辆位置确定感兴趣区域即车辆前脸区域,采用 2.4 节感兴趣区域定位的方法,对实验数据进行处理得到车辆前脸区域。考虑到车型识别的训练样本应覆盖多种光照条件、不同车辆姿态等图像样本,我们规定当所截取的车辆前脸图像与实际前脸包围框相差不超过 20% 时即可作为训练样本,如图 2-9 所示为几张正确获取 ROI 及偏差较大 ROI 图像示意图。通过对相同实验数据进行处理,能正确获取 ROI 的图像占所有测试图像的百分比为 95.33%,因此,该方法可以为车型识别提供实时准确的输入图像数据。

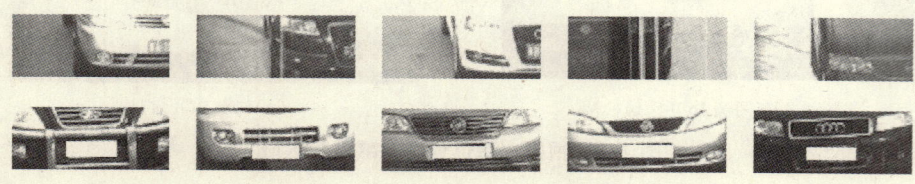

图 2-9 偏差较大 ROI 及正确获取 ROI,第一行为偏差加大 ROI,第二行为正确获取 ROI

2.2 特征描述器

所提出的车型识别系统包括两个步骤,第一步是从训练样本中提取特征训练分类器,第二步使用分类器对测试样本进行识别。图像特征提取应该能提供图像识别所需要的内在的、结构化的信息,现在有多种不同类型定义图像特征的方法。如图像颜色、灰度直方图、Gabor 滤波器和小波变换等方法。对于车辆图像来说,几何特征和边缘特征同等重要,如几何特征包括平方映射梯度[24]和梯度方向点[36]等。图像边缘的空间分布可以作为车辆识别有效的"指纹"信息。本章根据车辆类型识别需要引入两种边缘信息描述子,即 HOG 和 Contourlet 特征,为了避免维数灾难,论文提出使用主成分分析(PCA)进行数据降维,同时,本章探讨了使用特征融合提升识别率的可能性,并提出使用两种特征简单串联作为融合特征,在车型识别阶段通过实验分析了几种不同特征的识别效果。

2.2.1 梯度方向直方图(HOG)

梯度方向直方图(HOG)特征是由 Dalal[20]提出并应用于静态图像中的行人检测上,后来推广到静态图像中的车辆、行人及常见动物等目标的检测。该特征计算局部图像梯度的方向信息的统计值,与尺度不变特征变换(SIFT)、边缘方向直方图(EOH)以及形状上下文方法等特征在计算方法上有相似之处,但 HOG 描述器是在一个网格密集的大小统一的胞元(Cells)上计算,同时还采用了重叠的对比度归一化技术提高性能。HOG 的具体实现方法是:首先将图像分成小的连通区域,即细胞单元(Cells);然后根据 Cells 中各像素点的梯度方向和幅值计算得到其梯度方向直方图;最后把这些直方图组合起来构成特征描述器。为了提高性能,把这些 Cells 的梯度方向直方图在图像的更大区间(Block)内进行归一化,即先计算各直方图在区间中的密度,然后根据密度对区间中的各细胞单元进行归一化,通过归一化能够消除光照和阴影的影响。具体流程图如图 2-10 所示。

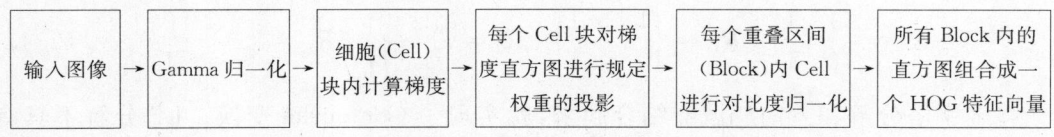

图 2-10 HOG 特征提取算法流程

2.2.2 Contourlet 变换

Contourlet 变换是结合拉普拉斯塔形分解(LP)和方向滤波器组(DFB)实现的一种多分辨率、多方向的、局域的图像表示方法,是由 Do[45]提出的。Contourlet 变换用随尺度变化长宽比的"长条形"基结构来逼近图像,具有方向性和各向异性。Contourlet 对曲线的表述如图 2-11 所示。

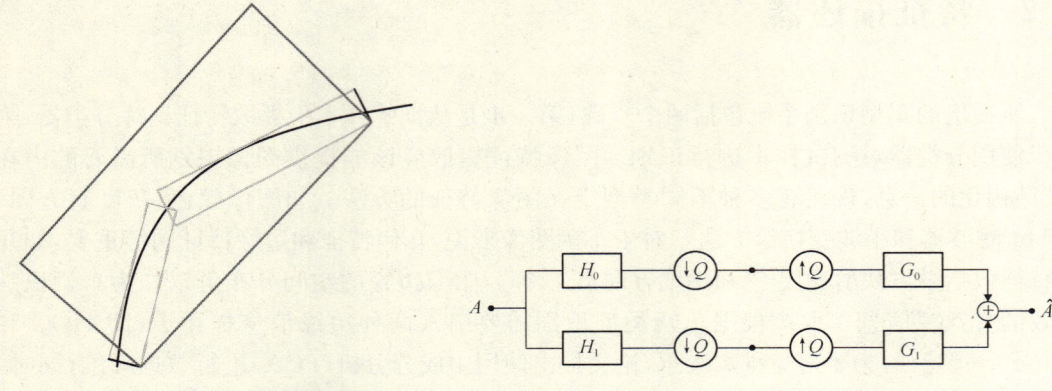

图 2-11　Contourlet 变换对曲线的描述　　图 2-12　Quincunx 滤波器

LP 分解是实现图像多分辨率分析的一种有效方式。每一层 LP 分解将产生一个下采样的低通部分和一个该图像与预测图像的差值图像。对低通图像继续分解得到下一层的低通图像和差值图像。二维方向滤波器组（DFB）应用于 LP 分解得到的每一级高频分量上，在第 l 层上得到 2^l 个方向子带,图像每次经 LP 子带分解产生的高通子带输入 DFB，逐渐将点奇异连成线结构，从而捕获图像中的轮廓。Do 提出的 DFB 包括两个模块，即梅花滤波器组和平移操作。两通道的梅花滤波器组（Quincunx 滤波器，如图 2-12 所示）是用扇形滤波器将 2-D 光谱分成两个主要方向，水平方向和垂直方向。其中，H 和 G 为分解和合成滤波，Q 为采样矩阵，有两种形式：

$$Q_0 = \begin{Bmatrix} 1 & -1 \\ 1 & 1 \end{Bmatrix} \quad Q_1 = \begin{Bmatrix} 1 & 1 \\ -1 & 1 \end{Bmatrix} \tag{2-12}$$

其中，Q 的作用是将图像旋转并下采样，Q_0 和 Q_1 分别将图像旋转 45°和 −45°。平移操作（Shearing）是在 Quincunx 滤波分解阶段前进行。Shearing 操作对图像进行旋转并将其宽度变为原来的两倍。Shearing 操作可采用如下四种采样矩阵：

$$R_0 = \begin{Bmatrix} 1 & 1 \\ 0 & 1 \end{Bmatrix} \quad R_1 = \begin{Bmatrix} 1 & -1 \\ 0 & 1 \end{Bmatrix} \quad R_2 = \begin{Bmatrix} 1 & 0 \\ 1 & 1 \end{Bmatrix} \quad R_3 = \begin{Bmatrix} 1 & 0 \\ -1 & 1 \end{Bmatrix} \tag{2-13}$$

将金字塔分解和方向滤波器结合起来，就实现了 Contourlet 变换。LP 分解不具有方向性，而 DFB 能够较好理解高频部分，对低频部分分析程度不够，二者的结合弥补了对方的不足，从而得到了很好的图像描述。图 2-13 显示了一幅输入车辆前脸图像的三层 Contourlet 分解，其中第 l 层分解的方向子带数为 2^l，最细致层上的方向子带数为 16，图中将每层的所有子带拼成了一张图片。在实际的车型识别过程中，将子带图像直接作为输入特征会造成特征向量维数过高，但直接将每个子带的均值和方差作为输入特征又会忽略掉比较多的细节信息，本文提出采用每一层所有子带合并后的图像的每行均值和方差作为特征，对于一张输入大小为 256×256 的图像，Contourlet 变换后的三层子带合并图像大小分别为 16×16，64×64，128×128。则该图像的 Contourlet 特征维数大小

为 $2\times(16+64+128)=896$。

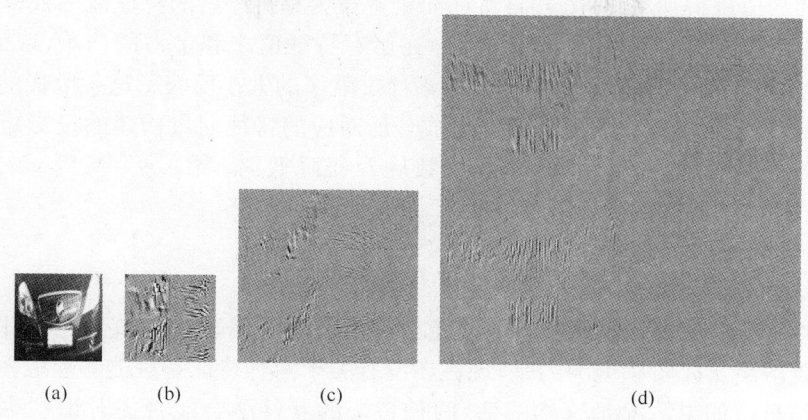

图 2-13 输入车辆图像的三层 Contourlet 分解

2.2.3 特征降维

在机器学习中,对于高维特征向量经常采用一些降低维数的方法来避免维数灾难[101],在训练样本固定的情况下,一些分类器(如贝叶斯网络、k 近邻)的预测能力通常随着特征向量维度的增加而减小。所以在将样本输入分类器之前通常采取一些降低维数的措施,降低特征向量维数的方法有主成分分析(PCA),线性判别分析(LDA)[102]和典型相关分析(CCA)[103]等,同时支持向量机(SVM)中的核函数[46]也可以有效地解决高维到低维的映射问题。

前两节所介绍的两种特征描述子提取出的图像特征维数都比较高,如不对获取的特征向量进行维数降低处理,那么分类器对信息处理的效率和精确度都会下降。主成分分析(PCA)是一个高普适用方法,通过 PCA 方法求出数据集的主元,将其余的维数省去,从而达到维数降低和简化模型的目的。PCA 方法是将数据空间通过正交变换映射到低维子空间的过程,通过求得一个低维的投影矩阵,用高维的特征乘以这个投影矩阵,便可以将高维特征的维数下降到指定的维数。假设有 N 个样本数据 $\boldsymbol{X}_i=\{x_1^i,x_2^i,\cdots,x_D^i\}$,$1\leqslant i\leqslant N$,其中 D 为样本特征维数,PCA 的目标是寻找 $r(r<D)$ 个新变量,使它们反映事物的主要特征,具体实现过程如下所述:

(1) 计算所有样本的均值向量

$$\mu=\left\{\frac{1}{N}\sum_{i=1}^{N}x_1^i,\ \frac{1}{N}\sum_{i=1}^{N}x_2^i,\ \cdots,\ \frac{1}{N}\sum_{i=1}^{N}x_D^i\right\} \quad (2\text{-}14)$$

(2) 计算协方差矩阵

$$S=\frac{1}{N}\sum_{i=1}^{N}[\boldsymbol{X}_i-\boldsymbol{u}][\boldsymbol{X}_i-\boldsymbol{u}]^{\mathrm{T}} \quad (2\text{-}15)$$

(3) 计算矩阵 S 的特征值 λ_i 和对应的特征向量 v_i；

(4) 对特征值进行递减排序，并将特征向量重排为和排序后的特征值一致；

(5) 定义贡献率为主要特征值（主成分）在所有特征值之和中占的比重，取前 r 个主要特征值（主成分）代替原来所有的特征值时，累计贡献率的大小反映了这种取代的可靠性。

(6) 最后，用输入特征向量乘以 r 个主成分所对应的特征向量构建的投影矩阵，即可达到数据维数降低的目的，将输入样本特征维数从 D 维降低到 r 维。

2.2.4 组合特征及降维

尽管现在 HOG 和 Contourlet 特征已经具有广泛的应用，但关于它们实用性的许多问题还没有得到解决。要特别说明的是，现在还没有关于两种特征是否能够获取图像潜在的、不同的互补信息。如果情况是这样的话，两种特征的互补融合能否提升识别率值得关注。从大体上来说，本文所提及的两种特征能够从不同角度描述图像内容，同时使用两种特征得到图像的综合信息来提升分类器识别车型的效率是个不错的选择。近年来也有些关于组合两种不同特征描述子的方法的研究。其中有一种广泛使用的是基于典型相关分析（CCA）[63] 的特征融合方法。但是 CCA 是一种无监督的特征提取方法并且它不采用样本的类型信息，这就限制了识别功能。另外一种颇具影响力的特征融合方法是支持向量机（SVM）框架中的多核学习[46]，这种方法通过线性组合来开发不同特征的核。基于核的方法相对于其他特征融合方法的最大优势是它能够组合不同来源数据的信息。由于我们所涉及的车型数据来源单一，所以本文使用了一种较为简单的特征组合方法。

如何有效地进行多特征融合仍是一个开放问题，但多特征融合能够提升系统的可靠性和健壮性已是学者们的共识。直接将两种特征如 HOG 和 Contourlet 特征简单串联是一种有效的提升识别率的方法，其中多层神经网络（MLP）对融合特征的识别效率的提升尤其显著，而且使用 MLP 多分类器集成和融合特征结合能够进一步提升识别率。本文所使用的第一个特征是 HOG 特征，将一幅输入图像归一化为 64×64，设置细胞单元大小为 8×8，在每个细胞单元内统计 9 个直方图通道的无向梯度（即将 $0 \sim 180°$ 的梯度方向划分为 9 个区间），同时设置归一化块（block）的大小为 16×16（即包含四个细胞单元），块在水平和竖直方向的步进大小均为 8，如图 2-14 所示为各尺寸之间的相对关系，最后将所有细胞单元的直方图组合起来形成 HOG 特征描述子，得到的特征描述子大小为 $9 \times 4 \times 7 \times 7 = 1764$。

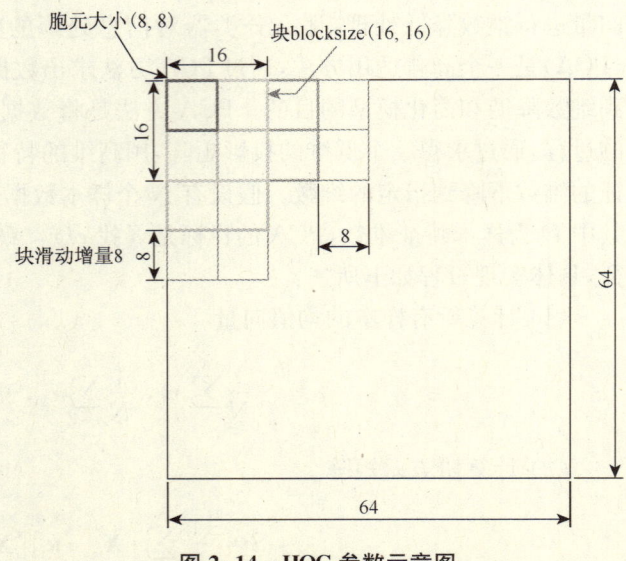

图 2-14　HOG 参数示意图

对于 Contourlet 特征,对输入车辆图片进行三层分解,将每一层对应的所有自带拼成一张图片,统计 Contourlet 在每层子带拼接图像的每行均值方差作为特征描述子。由于车辆图像横向信息存在冗余,将输入图像归一化为 256×256,则得到每层 Contourlet 分解子带拼接图像大小分别为 16×16,64×64 和 128×128,统计每行的均值方差作为特征描述子,最终得到特征向量的大小为 (64+128+256)×2 = 896 维。

分类器中朴素贝叶斯分类器和 k-近邻对高维特征都比较敏感,当维数比较高时,神经网络的参数设计也比较复杂,可能需要比较多的隐含层结点,训练时间也比较长,因此对特征进行降低维数是必要的。分别对 HOG 和 Contourlet 特征进行 PCA 分析,取累计贡献率为 95% 对应的投影矩阵,将训练样本和测试样本特征使用投影矩阵进行变换,得到投影后的 HOG 和 Contourlet 特征维数分别为 570 维和 130 维,对应之前的高维特征数据维数降低较为明显。

2.3 基于级联集成分类器的可靠分类

特征分类的过程是通过建立样本集经分类器学习后,可将输入测试样本自动分类到已知类别。模式识别中有很多成熟的分类器如神经网络,k-近邻和支持向量机[104],但现在关于分类器可靠性问题的研究还比较少,可靠性即分类器做出某个决定的置信度。尽管现在已有的分类器可以达到很高的识别效率,但是对于交通监控中嫌疑车辆的识别来说需要更高的可靠度。目前道路上运行的车辆类型很多,现在很难将所有的车型都包含在数据库中,对于未知车型的强行分类显得毫无意义;另外,在车辆检测过程中也无法做到每一辆车都能精确提取到感兴趣区域,将背景作为车辆区域进行分类显然会得到不好的结果。这时,如果能在分类器中加入"拒识"功能,即拒绝识别置信度不高的输入样本(模糊图片、新车型、背景区域等),而将这些样本拣出由人工识别,这样显然就提高了分类器的可靠性。本章首先介绍几种成熟的分类器,分别使用不同的分类器对两种特征和融合特征进行识别,同时引入一种带有"拒识"功能的级联集成分类器方案。

一个能够最小化错误率并且能将不确定类型的测试样本归属到"拒识"类中的分类器是衡量分类器是否最优的简单规则。Chow[52]提出了一个具有"拒识"功能的最优规则,它应满足下面两个条件:

对于一个输入样本向量 v,分类器对它识别并将其归属到第 k 类,根据贝叶斯公式,应满足:

$$p(k)p(v|k) \geqslant p(i)p(v|i) \tag{2-16}$$

$$p(k)p(v|k) \geqslant \rho \sum_{i=1, i \neq k}^{C} p(i)p(v|i) \tag{2-17}$$

在满足以下条件时,分类器拒绝识别输入样本向量 v:

$$\max_{k}[p(k)p(v|k)] \leqslant \rho \sum_{i=1, i \neq k}^{C} p(i)p(v|i) \tag{2-18}$$

其中 C 为类型数目，$p(i)$（$i=1,\cdots,C$）为每一类的先验概率，$p(v|i)$ 为给定类型的条件概率，可以根据输入样本计算得到，在决策规则中的 ρ 被称为"决策阈值"，且 $0 \leqslant \rho \leqslant 1$。降低"拒识"率及错误率的方法有以下几种：

（1）为了降低错误率，我们需要通过增加公式(4-2)和(4-3)中的 ρ 来扩大"拒绝区域"。这样，被拒绝的样本会增多而被正确或错误识别的样本都会减少。

（2）根据公式(4-3)为了降低"拒识"率，首先可以通过提高 $\max[p(k)p(v|k)]$ 的值，在此同时可以降低 $\rho \sum_{i=1; i \neq k}^{C} p(i)p(v|i)$ 的值。这就是说，在实际的识别过程中，一个输入样本应该具有与其对应类型最高的条件概率，并且相对于其他类型的条件概率最小。这意味着能够有效描述图像的特征在识别过程中扮演重要的角色。

引入"拒识"功能后，我们采用[54]中的方法如下定义识别率(Recognition Rate，RR)，"拒识"率(Rejection Rate，ReR)，错误率(Error Rate，ER)以及系统可靠性：

$$RR = \frac{正确识别的样本数}{所有测试样本数} \quad (2\text{-}19)$$

$$ReR = \frac{"拒识"的样本数}{所有测试样本数} \quad (2\text{-}20)$$

$$可靠性 = RR + ReR \quad (2\text{-}21)$$

$$ER = 100\% - 可靠性 \quad (2\text{-}22)$$

根据识别系统可靠性的定义，在合适权衡"拒识"率(ReR)和错误率(ER)之间的关系后，我们可以得到一个可靠性比较高的车型识别系统。

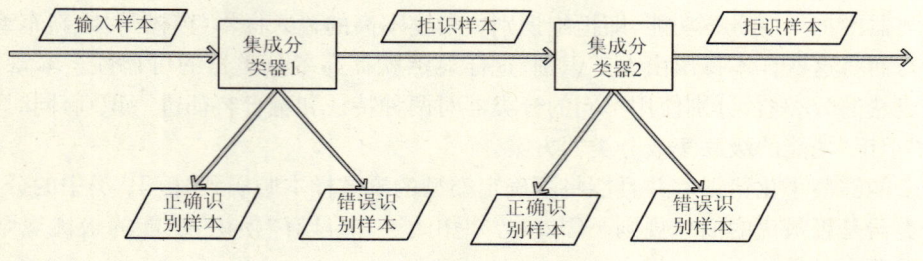

图 2-15 级联集成分类器方案

分类器集成的思想是分别训练一系列单个的分类器，之后选择合适的方法组合它们的分类结果。集成分类器不仅仅依靠某一单一训练集的特点，还要能够学习样本更具表现力的内容，以解决单个分类器的分类偏好问题。建立集成分类器有很多方法。一个主流的方法是分别使用训练样本的不同子集训练每个分类器，可以通过对训练数据重新采样(Bagging)[48]、赋予新权值(Boosting)[49]来实现。Bagging（"bootstrap aggregation"的简称）使用一种统计重采样技术"bootstrap"生成多个训练子集和集成分类器中的分类器组件。Boosting 的每个分类器组件的训练样本是由在它之前的分类器决定的，在前一个分类器中被误分的样本将在下一个分类器中扮演重要的角色。另外一个比较有前景的集成分类器是随机子空间(Random Subspace)[51],它使用从所有特征中随机选取的子集作为训练样本。因此,集成分类器是由基分类器使用特征空间中随机选取的特征子集进行训练实现的。本节我们介绍一个通过降低"拒识"率及提高识别率来实现一个高可靠性的分类系统的集成分类器级联方案。多层识别系统可以由若干个两级级联识别系统组成,因此我们仅介绍一个两级级联方案。如图 2-15 所示,第二级的集成分类器的输入测试样本是在第一级级联分类器中被拒绝识别的样本。

对于两层集成分类器,相应的识别率,"拒识"率和误识率满足以下关系:

$$总识别率 = \frac{第一级识别数 + 第二级识别数}{总样本数};$$

$$总误识率 = \frac{第一级误识数 + 第二级误识数}{总样本数};$$

$$第二级"拒识"率 = \frac{第一级"拒识"数 - 第二级误识数 - 第二级识别数}{第一级"拒识"数}。$$

相对于单级的集成分类器,经过两级级联的处理,被"拒识"的样本会减少。即两级的"拒识"率小于单级的"拒识"率。另外两级级联的识别率要高于单级分类器的识别率,同时,两级级联的误识率要高于单级的误识率。

本文所分析的级联分类器的第一级是由四种不同的分类器(朴素贝叶斯,kNN,MLP 及 SVM)集成,分别使用朴素贝叶斯、k-近邻(kNN)、多层神经网络(MLP)及支持向量机(SVM)对输入的 HOG 和 Contourlet 特征进行训练,训练后得到 8 组决策机制。级联分类器的第二级是使用旋转森林(Rotation Forest)并以 MLP 作为基分类器实现,以下就两级级联分类器的原理及方案分别介绍。

本节将首先分析朴素贝叶斯、k-近邻(kNN)、多层神经网络(MLP)及支持向量机(SVM)共四种分类器的原理,并使用两种输入特征进行训练得到 8 组决策机制,之后使用 8 组决策机制进行投票的方式构建集成分类器对输入测试样本进行表决,表决通过的样本分为正确识别和错误识别两类样本,表决没有通过即 8 种机制未达成一致的样本将送入下一级集成分类器进行识别。

1) 朴素贝叶斯分类器

对于一个二值分类问题,设样本由 n 维特征向量 $x(x \in R^n)$ 和类型值 y ($y \in C$) 表示,其中 $C = \{-1, +1\}$。根据贝叶斯定理,后验概率如下定义:

$$p(C_i \mid x) = \frac{p(C_i)p(x \mid C_i)}{p(x)}, \quad i = 1, 2 \tag{2-23}$$

其中,$p(C_i)$ 为类型值 C_i 的先验概率,$p(x \mid C_i)$ 是给定类型值 C_i 下 x 的条件概率,$p(x) = \sum_{i=1}^{2} p(C_i)p(x \mid C_i)$ 为 x 的边缘概率或证据。

朴素贝叶斯分类假设特征向量的每个属性是条件独立的,根据贝叶斯定理可给出朴素贝叶斯的定义:设 $X = \{x_1, x_2, \cdots, x_n\}$ 为某待分类样本的特征向量,n 为特征维数,其中每个 $x_i(1 \leqslant i \leqslant n)$ 为一个特征属性,特征对应的类别集合为 $C = \{c_1, c_2, \cdots, c_m\}$,$m$ 为

类型值个数,则根据贝叶斯定理,给定特征 X 下的类型值的条件概率 p 为:

$$p(C_k \mid x_1, x_2, \cdots, x_n) = \frac{p(x_1, x_2, \cdots, x_n \mid C_i) p(C_i)}{p(x_1, x_2, \cdots, x_n)}, \quad (1 \leqslant k \leqslant m) \quad (2\text{-}24)$$

其中用于计算的证据 $p(x_1, x_2, \cdots, x_n)$ 是相同的,我们不考虑这个条件,如果有很多类型,则需要找到分子最大的才能实现分类。分子是特征的类型值和特征向量的联合概率:$p(C_i, x_1, x_2, \cdots, x_n)$,重复使用链式法则,可以使用条件概率表示这个联合概率:

$$\begin{aligned}
& p(C_k, x_1, x_2, \cdots, x_n) \\
&= p(C_k) p(x_1, x_2, \cdots, x_n \mid C_k) \\
&= p(C_k) p(x_1 \mid C_k) p(x_2, x_3, \cdots, x_n \mid C_k, x_1) \\
&= p(C_k) p(x_1 \mid C_k) p(x_2 \mid C_k, x_1) p(x_3, x_4, \cdots, x_n \mid C_k, x_1, x_2) \\
&= p(C_k) p(x_1 \mid C_k) p(x_2 \mid C_k, x_1) p(x_3 \mid C_k, x_1, x_2) \cdots p(x_n \mid C_k, x_1, x_2, \cdots, x_{n-1})
\end{aligned} \quad (2\text{-}25)$$

基于"朴素"条件独立的假设,每个特征 x_i 相对于其他特征 $x_j (j \neq i)$ 是条件独立的,即 $p(x_i \mid C, x_j) = p(x_i \mid C)$,所以对于 $i \neq j$,联合概率模型可以表示为

$$\begin{aligned}
p(C_k, x_1, x_2, \cdots, x_n) &= p(C_k) p(x_1 \mid C_k) p(x_2 \mid C_k) p(x_3 \mid C_k) \cdots \\
&= p(C_k) \prod_{i=1}^{n} p(x_i \mid C_k)
\end{aligned} \quad (2\text{-}26)$$

式(2-26)即为朴素贝叶斯分类器模型,使用这个分类器的时候,需要学习车辆类型对应的类型值,计算每个类别在训练样本中的出现频率以及每个特征属性划分对每个类别的条件概率估计,并将结果记录。识别过程中,对于输入向量 X 使用(2-26)寻找联合概率最大时对应的类型值,即可实现样本自动分类。

2) k-近邻分类器

k-近邻分类算法是所有的机器学习算法中最简单的算法之一:给定一个常数 K,若某个样本在特征空间中的 K 个最相似样本中大多数属于某一类,则将输入样本分配给该类。判断相似度的规则一般使用欧拉距离,已知样本特征集合 D,其中包含 m 个样本,对于某一特定的输入特征向量 $X = \{x_1, x_2, \cdots, x_n\}$,使用 k-近邻分类的算法是:

(1) 使用欧拉公式计算输入特征与特征集合中 m 个样本的欧拉距离

$$g_i = \| X - D_i \| = \sqrt{\sum_{j=1}^{n} (x_j - d_j)^2}, \quad 1 \leqslant i \leqslant m \quad (2\text{-}27)$$

(2) 将 $g_i (1 \leqslant i \leqslant m)$ 从小到大排序,并根据设定的常数 K 取前 K 个最相似的样本;

(3) 采用投票表决的方式确定最终的分类结果,在 K 个最相似样本中寻找最多的某一类对应的类型值,这里的 K 一般取奇数,避免两种票数相等难以决策。

3) 多层神经网络(MLP)

人工神经网络充分吸收了人识别物体的特点,除了图像本身的统计、空间几何特征,它在被分类图像特征信息的指导下,通过自学习,修改网络结构及识别方式,达到提高分类精

度和速度的目的。目前,在模式识别中使用最多的为多层前馈网络,其中又以 BP 网络为代表。BP(Back-Propagation)网络即反向传播算法,其实质是使用非线性优化问题解决样本输入输出之间关系映射问题,并通过梯度下降算法结合迭代运算来求解网络传播权值的一种学习方法。BP 神经网络的模型如图 2-16 所示:

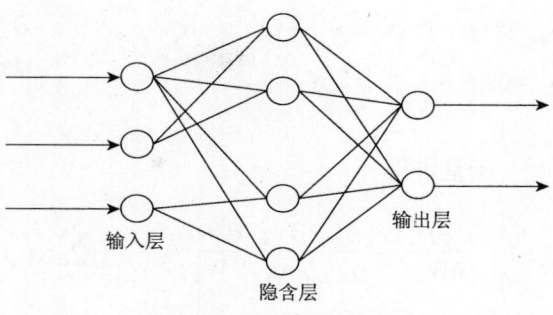

图 2-16 BP 网络模型

BP 网络通常选用三层结构,除了输入层、输出层结点,还可增加一个到多个隐含层结点,但增加网络层数并不能提升网络的分类能力。对于输入信号,要先向前传播到隐含层结点,经过作用函数后,再把隐含层结点的输出信号传播到输出结点,最后得到输出结果,映射函数一般采用 Sigmoid 函数:

$$f(x) = \frac{1}{1+e^{-x}} \tag{2-28}$$

BP 算法的实质是一个均方最小误差问题,对于训练样本 $X(x_k, k=1, 2, \cdots, n)$,期望输出为 $t=(t_1, t_2, \cdots, t_c)$,实际输出为 $z=(z_1, z_2, \cdots, z_c)$,隐含层输出为 $y=(y_1, y_2, \cdots, y_h)$,其中 c 为输出层结点个数,h 为隐含层结点个数,第 k 个神经元的输出为 net_k。则 BP 算法的目标函数为最小化误差函数:

$$J = \frac{1}{2}\sum_{i=1}^{c}(t_i - z_i)^2 \tag{2-29}$$

权值的迭代公式为

$$W_{ij} = W_{ij} - \mu \frac{\partial J}{\partial W_{ij}} \tag{2-30}$$

其中,μ 为学习速率,$\mu > 0$。对于输出层结点,定义 $\delta_k = \frac{\partial J}{\partial net_k}$,于是

$$\frac{\partial J}{\partial W_{ij}} = \frac{\partial J}{\partial net_k}\frac{\partial net_k}{\partial W_{ij}} = \frac{\partial J}{\partial net_k}y_j = \delta_k y_j \tag{2-31}$$

$$\delta_k = \frac{\partial J}{\partial net_{jk}} = \frac{\partial J}{\partial z_k}\frac{\partial z_k}{\partial net_k} = -(t_k - z_k)f'(net_k) \tag{2-32}$$

对于非输出层结点,即隐含层结点,有

$$\frac{\partial J}{\partial y_j} = \frac{\partial}{\partial y_j}\left[\frac{1}{2}\sum_{k=1}^{c}(t_k - z_k)^2\right] = -\sum_{k=1}^{c}(t_k - z_k)\frac{\partial z_k}{\partial y_j}$$

$$= -\sum_{k=1}^{c}(t_k - z_k)\frac{\partial z_k}{\partial net_k}\frac{net_k}{\partial y_j} = -\sum_{k=1}^{c}(t_k - z_k)f'(net_k)W_{kj}$$
(2-33)

于是可得

$$\frac{\partial J}{\partial W_{ji}} = \frac{\partial J}{\partial y_j}\frac{\partial y_j}{\partial net_j}\frac{\partial net_j}{W_{ji}} = -\left[\sum_{k=1}^{c}(t_k - z_k)f'(net_k)W_{kj}\right]f'(net_k)x_i = \delta_j x_i$$
(2-34)

$$\delta_j = \frac{\partial J}{\partial net_j} = \frac{\partial J}{\partial y_j}\frac{\partial y_j}{\partial net_j} = f'(net_k)\sum_{k=1}^{c}\delta_k W_{kj}$$
(2-35)

BP 网络算法的学习过程由正向传播和反向传播组成,对于具有 M 层的 BP 网络来说,设置网络的初始权值 W 后,对于所有样本 $k=1,\cdots,N$,首先正向计算隐含层输出 y,神经元输出 net_k 和网络实际输出 z;然后对各层从 M 到 2 进行反向计算,用式(2-31)和(2-34)计算 δ_j,之后根据权值迭代公式(2-30)修正权值,直至网络收敛。

4) 支持向量机(SVM)

支持向量机(SVM)是 Cortes 和 Vapnik[54]首次提出的,它在解决小样本、非线性及高维数等方面表现出较大的优势。对于两类的情况,支持向量机假设训练集可被一个超平面线性划分,对于 n 维输入特征向量 x 和标记 $y = \{-1, +1\}$,定义一个点到超平面的间隔为

$$\delta_i = y_i(wx_i + b)$$
(2-36)

设 H_1 和 H_2 分别为各类中离超平面最近的样本且平行于分类超平面的平面,对于线性可分的情况,假设

$$\begin{cases} H_1: wx_i + b \geqslant 1, & y_i = 1 \\ H_2: wx_i + b \leqslant -1, & y_i = -1 \end{cases}$$
(2-37)

将 w 和 b 进行归一化,可得分类间隔为 $\frac{2}{\|w\|}$,使得分类间隔最大,使 $\frac{\|w\|}{2}$ 最小的超平面即为最优分类超平面,如图 2-17 所示,H 是分类面,H_1 和 H_2 平行于 H,且过离 H 最近的两类样本的点的直线,在 H_1 和 H_2 上的样本点即支持矢量。

为了避免所有样本点都集中到 H_1 和 H_2 之间的无法分类地带,将最小分类间隔 y_i 固定为 1,则问题转化为具有目标函数和约束条件的二次规划问题:

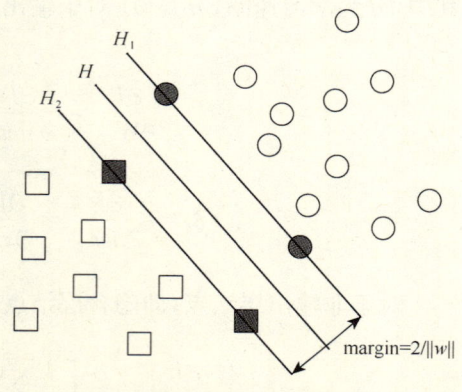

图 2-17 最优分类超平面

$$\begin{cases} \min \dfrac{\|w\|}{2} \\ y_i(wx_i+b) \geqslant 1, \ i=1,2,\cdots,n \end{cases} \tag{2-38}$$

通常求解上述问题的想法是使用非负拉格朗日乘子 α_i，得到该问题的对偶问题：

$$\min\left\{\dfrac{1}{2}\|w\|^2 - \sum_{i=1}^{n}\alpha_i[y_i(wx_i+b)-1]\right\} \tag{2-39}$$

为了避免通过将 α_i 趋向于 $+\infty$ 得到最小值，而不是原问题的最优解，忽略能够被 $y_i(wx_i+b)-1\geqslant 0$ 分离的点，设置相应的 α_i 为零，只有少部分 α_i 不为零，这些点即位于平面 H_1 和 H_2 上的样本点，对应的 x_i 即为支持矢量。则向量 w 为训练向量的线性组合，对应的 b 亦可求得：

$$w^* = \sum_{i=1}^{n}\alpha_i y_i x_i \tag{2-40}$$

$$b^* = y_i - w^* x_i \tag{2-41}$$

对应输入的测试样本 x，此时分类决策函数为

$$g(x) = \langle w^*, x\rangle + b^* = \sum_{i=1}^{n}\alpha_i y_i \langle x_i, x\rangle + b^* \tag{2-42}$$

对于非线性情况，需要采用满足 Mercer 条件的核函数（kernel function）将输入向量映射到一个高维特征空间中，核函数对应某一空间中的内积：

$$K(x_i, x_j) = \psi(x_i)\cdot\psi(x_j) \tag{2-43}$$

此时相应的决策函数为

$$g(x) = \sum_{i=1}^{n}\alpha_i y_i K(x_i, x_j) + b^* \tag{2-44}$$

第一级集成分类器基于简单的概念建立具有"拒识"功能的分类器："拒识"并没有正误之分，只是分类器对当前的输入样本保持中立的态度。我们通过使用上述四种不同的分类器对两种不同的输入特征进行训练建立集成分类器，对于某个置信度不够高的输入样本集成分类器将放弃对它的识别。使用八种分类机制对每个输入样本进行投票表决，建立具有"拒识"功能的集成分类器如图 2-18 所示。

对于一个给定的测试样本 $x\ (x\in R^n)$，集成分类器中每个决策机制将得出一个识别结果。假设集合中分类器的个数为 M_1，每个分类器预测的结果分别为 $l_1, l_2, \cdots, l_{M_1}$。在从 M_1 个分类结果决策时，样本最终类型是由所有分类器投票决定，当最少有 t 个分类器同意某一分类结果时，才将样本赋予该值，其中 t 的一种取法可以为：

$$t \geqslant \begin{cases} \dfrac{M_1}{2}+1, & M_1 \text{ 为偶数} \\ \dfrac{M_1+1}{2}, & M_1 \text{ 为奇数} \end{cases} \tag{2-45}$$

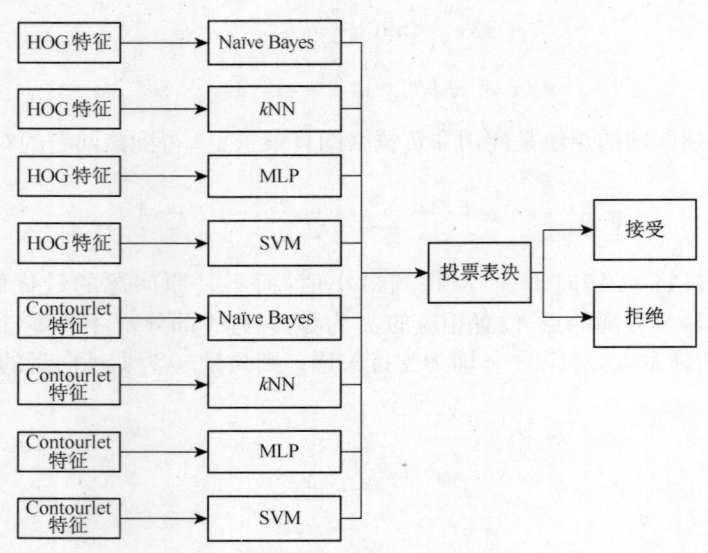

图 2-18　集成分类器表决机制

在其他情况下，集成分类器放弃对样本的识别。当进行多类样本分类时，只有当大多数分类器是正确时才进行分类，当大多数分类器结果不统一时放弃分类。如前所述，我们希望构建一个高可靠性、低"拒识"率、低误识率的分类器，为了达到降低"拒识"率的目的，将第一级被"拒识"的样本送入第二级进行再次识别。根据第一级集成分类器相同的理念，第二级分类器仍采用集成分类器来实现表决的目的。与第一级使用不同的基分类器进行集成不同，第二级采用相同的基分类器集成。我们选取多层神经网络（MLP）作为第二级的基分类器，这首先是基于提供充足的隐含层结点 MLP 可以拟合任何连续函数的考虑。另外，神经网络对不同的网络结构及输入特征向量一般具有不稳定的输出。

MLP 集成分类器得益于不同的基分类器对输入测试样本有不同的反映，为了进一步提升基分类器的多样性，我们使用一种新的被称为"元学习"算法的分类器集成方法——旋转森林（RF）[105]。与随机森林类似，旋转森林通过使用旋转特征空间来建立每一个基分类器。首先将输入特征集 F 划分为 K 个特征子集，然后对 K 个特征子集分别进行线性变换。之后使用 MLP 结合变换后的特征子集进行训练建立基分类器，这里线性变换的方法采用 PCA 分析。每次经过随机分割后得到的数据都被变换到不同的空间中，因而形成差别较大的分类子集。MLP 使用这些子集进行训练可以得到差异性较大的分类器，这样就进一步提升了集成分类器中 MLP 的多样性。

第二级集成分类器的表决机制如图 2-19 所示，与第一级集成分类器类似，最终样本类别由多个 MLP 通过投票决定。假设集成分类器中基分类器的个数为 M_2，当最少有 t 个分类器同意某一分类结果时，将输入测试样本类型值赋予该分类结果。这里的 t 是决策阈值，当 M_2 是偶数时 $t \geq \frac{M_2}{2}+1$，M_2 是奇数时 $t \geq \frac{M_2+1}{2}$。如果分类器对某样本的预测没有达成一致，则仍然拒绝对它的识别，显然这里 t 仍是决定"拒识"率的阈值。

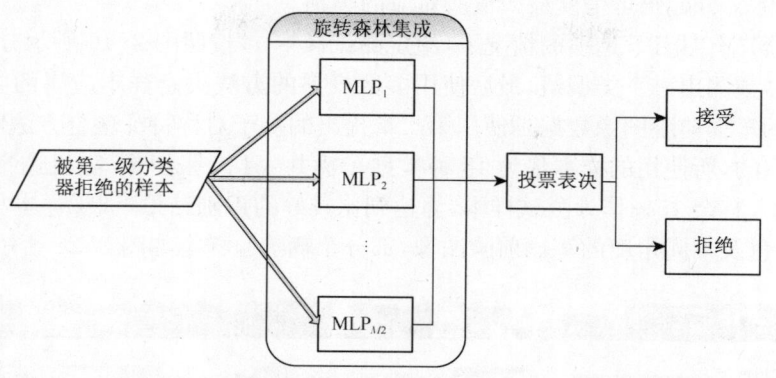

图 2-19　基于 MLP 的旋转森林集成分类器

旋转森林的实现原理为：给定包含 N 个样本的训练特征集 X，每个训练样本特征向量为 $x = \{x_1, \cdots, x_n\}$，其中 n 为特征向量维数。对应特征向量的类型值分别为 $y = \{y_1, \cdots, y_N\}$，其中 y_i 的值为 $\omega_1, \cdots, \omega_C$ 中的一个，C 为类型总数。F 表示特征集。使用 $D_1, \cdots, D_L$ 表示每个基分类器，L 为基分类器个数，每个基分类器并行地进行训练。对于每个基分类器 D_i，按照以下步骤生成训练集：

1) 设定参数 K，将 F 随机分为 K 个特征子集，特征子集可以互不相交或有交错。为了最大化多样性，我们选择互不相交的特征子集。K 通常设为维数 n 的因子，则每个特征子集包含的特征个数为 $M = n/K$。

2) 设 F_{ij} 为基分类器 D_i 的第 j 个特征子集，X_{ij} 为 X 中只包含 F_{ij} 的特征子集，对于每个特征子集进行随机不放回抽取 75% 的样本得到样本子集 X'_{ij}。对 X'_{ij} 进行 PCA 分析并存储主成分系数，即特征向量 $a_{ij}^{(1)}, \cdots, a_{ij}^{(M_j)}$，由于求取的协方差矩阵的特征值有些为 0，则 $M_j \leqslant M$。

3) 将对 K 个特征子集进行主成分分析得到的系数向量使用一个稀疏"旋转"矩阵 R_i 表示：

$$R_i = \begin{bmatrix} a_{ij}^{(1)}, \cdots, a_{ij}^{(M_1)} & [0] & \cdots & [0] \\ [0] & a_{ij}^{(1)}, \cdots, a_{ij}^{(M_2)} & \cdots & [0] \\ \vdots & \vdots & \ddots & \vdots \\ [0] & [0] & \cdots & a_{ij}^{(1)}, \cdots, a_{ij}^{(M_k)} \end{bmatrix} \quad (2\text{-}46)$$

旋转矩阵 R_i 的维数为 $n \times \sum_j M_j$。由于旋转矩阵的特征顺序在随机抽样的过程中被打乱，在计算分类器 D_i 的训练特征之前，需要将 R_i 按原始的特征顺序重排，重排后得到的旋转矩阵为 R_i^a。则分类器 D_i 的训练样本为 XR_i^a。训练完分类器后，在没有"拒识"的情况下，给定测试样本 x，假设 $d_{i,j}(xR_i)$ 为分类器 D_i 判断其为 ω_j 类的概率，则样本分配给每个类别 ω_j 的可信度为

$$u_j(x) = \frac{1}{L} \sum_{i=1}^{L} d_{i,j}(xR_i), \quad j = 1, \cdots, C \quad (2\text{-}47)$$

4) 最后将 x 分配给可信度最大值所对应的类别。

在分类器具有"拒识"选项的情况下,给定测试样本 x,按照图 2-19 所示分类决策方案,每个基分类器预测出一个类型值,最后使用多数投票的方法决定样本应属的类型。本部分实验所使用的车辆前脸图像数据是使用第二章提出的基于对称特征融合方法对输入样本进行处理所获取的,所使用的样本集为 18 种类型车辆共 4 140 张图像,随机选择其中的 85%作为训练样本,其余 15%作为测试样本,为达到比较好的识别结果,训练样本尽可能包含了各种光照、颜色及不同角度的车辆前脸图像,部分车辆前脸样本如图 2-20 所示。

图 2-20　部分车辆前脸图像

2.4　实验分析

本文所涉及的模式识别算法由 OpenCV 中机器学习(ML)[106]库实现,ML 库中集成了 Boosting、随机森林、神经网络等成熟算法,我们根据 ML 库中算法对输入输出特征向量的要求设置相应的参数,如神经网络中设置输入节点个数为特征向量维数,输出节点个数与类型个数相等,根据上一章所述方法设置中间层节点个数,训练步长为 1 000,训练误差收敛时小于 0.000 1,其他算法所使用的参数在以下内容有详细介绍。本文所有程序在 VS2008 下实现,所使用电脑为研华工控机,配置为 Intel Core Duo2.0 GHz。

在实验中不同分类器的参数设置介绍如下。对于朴素贝叶斯分类器,分别计算训练样本中特征向量每个特征对于类型值的条件概率以及每个类别的先验概率,对测试样本使用联合概率计算公式(2-26)寻找联合概率最大时对应的类型值,实现样本的自动分类。对于 kNN 分类器,在保证 k 为奇数和投票表决公正的条件下,设置 k 的大小为9。

对于多层神经网络(MLP)分类器,实验中设计了一个三层的 BP 网络,其中输入层结点个数 n_i 为样本特征向量维数,输出层结点个数 n_o 为车辆类型总数18,因此需要建立一个大小为18维的矢量,在神经网络的训练模式中,首选是"双极"模式,我们使用 0.5 赋值给相应位置的模式,其他位置被赋值为 -0.5,比如说第 8 类车辆对应的神经网络输出向量为

$$\begin{Bmatrix} -0.5, -0.5, -0.5, -0.5, -0.5, -0.5, \\ -0.5, 0.5, -0.5, -0.5, -0.5, -0.5, \\ -0.5, -0.5, -0.5, -0.5, -0.5, -0.5 \end{Bmatrix} \tag{2-48}$$

从向量(2-48)中可以看出,输出向量只有第 8 个位置被设置成 0.5,其余都为 -0.5。根据经验[107],网络隐含层结点个数 n_h 取

$$n_h = \sqrt{n_i + n_o} + m \tag{2-49}$$

其中,m 为常数,且 $m \in [1, 10]$。在支持向量机(SVM)分类器中,我们使用了线性核函数进行特征从低维到高维的映射,线性核函数的表示形式为

$$K(x_i, x_j) = x_i^T \cdot x_j \tag{2-50}$$

在本文所使用的四种分类器中,只有 MLP 的输出标签是特征向量,其他三种分类器所对应的样本特征值分别为 0 到 17 的 18 个整数。

2.4.1 单个分类器实验

对于所有的分类检测实验,我们每种车型随机选择 200 张图片作为训练样本,其余 30 张作为测试样本。第一个实验是对不同分类器使用不同特征进行训练的识别结果的比较,按照之前所述的,使用两种特征以及它们的简单串联融合特征进行实验,每种分类机制所对应的识别结果如图 2-21 和表 2.2 所示。

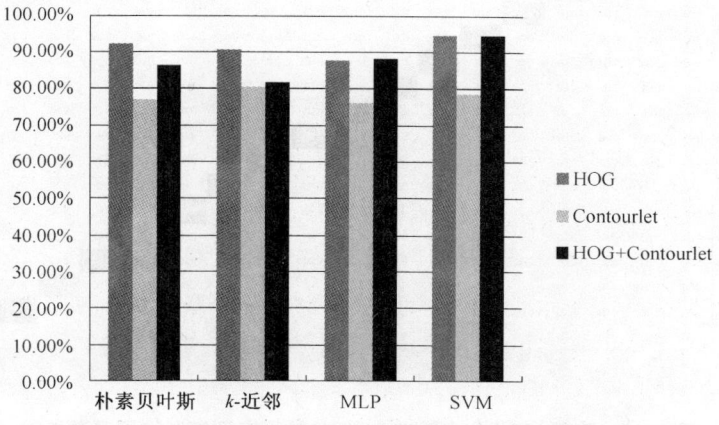

图 2-21 四种分类器和两种特征的分类识别结果比较

表 2.2 朴素贝叶斯、k-近邻、MLP 和 SVM 结合 HOG、Contourlet 特征分类

特征 \ 分类器	朴素贝叶斯	k-近邻	MLP	SVM
HOG	92.4%	90.6%	89.6%	94.6%
Contourlet	77.0%	80.4%	76.3%	78.5%
HOG+Contourlet	86.3%	81.7%	90.6%	94.6%

观察结果我们可以得到如下结论:

1) 首先,HOG 特征较之于 Contourlet 特征能够提取车辆图像较为丰富的信息并能提供不同车型更具分辨力的特征,因为由结果中可以看出四种分类器——朴素贝叶斯、k-近邻、MLP 和 SVM 使用 HOG 特征都得到了比较好的结果。

2) 其次,使用 SVM 作为分类器,较之于其他分类器的识别结果最好。

3) 最后,简单地使用两种特征的串联特征作为融合特征对于朴素贝叶斯分类器,kNN 和 SVM 来说并不能显著提高识别效果,甚至还会使识别效果变差,论文[108]中提到了这种现象。这可能是由于不同的特征描述子提供不相同的信息,特征向量元素之间并不平衡,简单串联两种特征对多数分类器来说效果并不好。比较好的方法是保存两种特征之间的关联信息。MLP 似乎能通过将两种特征进行非线性组合得到关键特征,并且通过调节隐含层结点和网络结构能够较好的提取两种特征之间的互补关系,进而得到较好的识别结果,给这种说法以严格证明还有一定难度。

在多类分类问题中,通常使用混淆矩阵对每一类的识别效果及每一类与其他类别的相似性进行分析,混淆矩阵的行和列分别为样本实际和预测的类型,对角线上的元素为每一类样本正确识别的概率,非对角线上的元素为该类识别成其他类型的概率,HOG 特征使用 SVM 分类器训练得到的分类器对测试样本的识别效果最好,对其进行分析,得到对应样本识别结果的混淆矩阵如图 2-22 所示。从图 2-22 可得,18 种类型车辆有 8 种车型的识别率

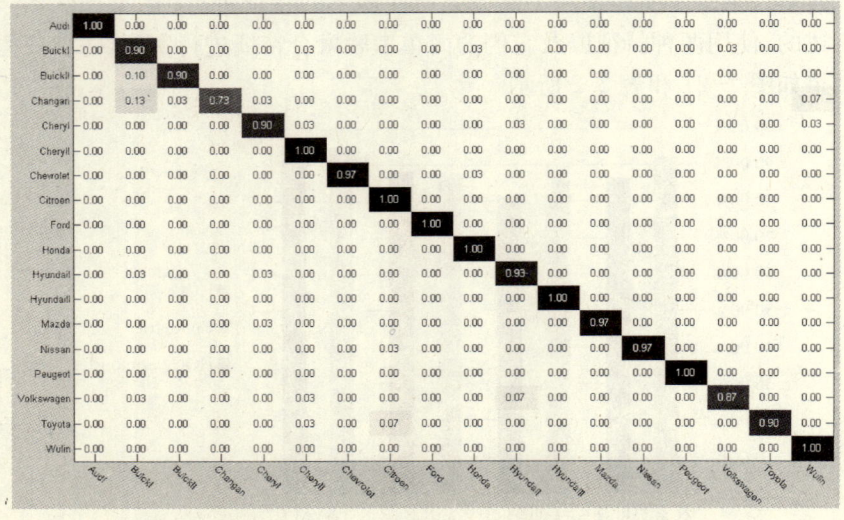

图 2-22 使用 SVM 分类器结合 HOG 特征车型识别结果混淆矩阵

为100%,包括 Audi,Chery II 型及 Citroen 等。其中 Changan、Chery I 型的识别率比较低,图 2-23 分别为 Chery I 型识别成 Chery II 型、Hyundai 及 Wulin 车的例图,其中所列的例图只是该种车型的代表。

从 2-23 可得,被错误识别的车辆存在几个问题:一是与其他类型车辆相似度比较高,如图 2-23(a)两种车型具有相同的散热器;二是光照条件的影响,如 2-23(b)中车辆图像是晚间拍摄,边缘细节信息已经模糊,对识别显然有影响;三是截取感兴趣区域的位置,如果所截取的车辆前脸区域包含较多的非车辆区域,则会对车型的识别产生影响。对于第一个问题,需要有能够描述车辆更详细的特征,例如 HOG and Contourlet 的融合特征,对于第二个和第三个问题,可以使用本文所提出的"拒识"方式来避免,即放弃对模糊车辆和包含非车辆区域图像的识别,以提高系统的可靠性,"拒识"方法在级联集成分类器中会有进一步的分析。

(a) Chery I 识别为 Hyundai

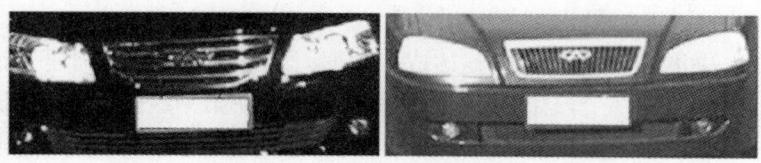

(b) Chery I 识别为 Chery II

(c) Chery I 识别为 Wulin

图 2-23 Chery I 型车识别成其他类型车辆例图,第一列为原车型,第二列为识别目标类型

2.4.2 级联集成分类器实验

进一步的实验是采用本文中所提出的级联集成分类器方法进行带有"拒识"功能的分类实验,即放弃对置信度不高的输入样本的识别。根据两级集成分类器级联方案,首先将输入样本送入级联分类器的第一级即具有不同基分类器的集成分类器中识别,之后将被第一级集成分类器"拒识"的样本送入级联的第二级分类器进行进一步识别,表 2.3 和图 2-24 为两级级联分类器及整个识别系统的识别率及可靠性关系柱状图。

表 2.3 两层级联分类器对样本识别指标

	识别率(RR)	拒识样本数	误识样本数	拒识率(ReR)	可靠性
第一级	76.30%	127	1	23.52%	99.80%
第二级	62.99%	38	9	29.92%	92.91%
识别系统	91.11%	38	10	7.04%	98.15%

根据之前的介绍,在级联的第一级中,集成分类器中有 8 种分类机制,即分别使用朴素贝叶斯、kNN、MLP 和 SVM 结合 HOG 和 Contourlet 特征进行训练。分类识别最终结果是根据 8 种决策机制进行 $k/8$ 多数投票决定,其中 k 为对测试样本接受识别和拒绝识别的阈值,根据之前所述的表决方法,我们取 $k=6$,即当有 6 种分类决策机制达成一致时接受对该样本的识别,否则拒绝对该样本的识别。使用上一节相同的实验数据进行分类识别,对 8 种决策机制的识别结果进行统计分

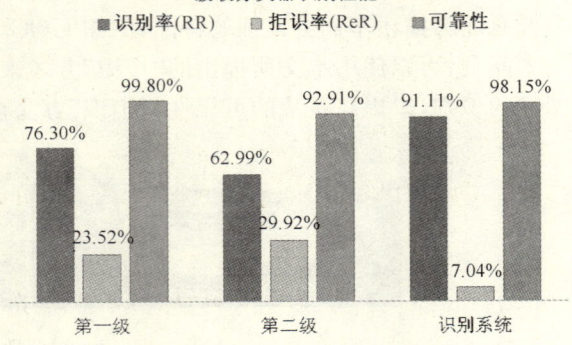

图 2-24 级联分类器的识别性能指标

析,当有 6 种以上决策机制的识别标签达成一致时,则将对应的样本归属于该类车辆。18 种车型每种测试样本为 30 个,总共有 540 个测试样本。在第一级被拒绝识别的样本为 127 个,识别错误的样本为 1 个。则被拒绝识别的样本占总样本的百分比即"拒识"率(ReR)为 23.52%,检测错误率(ER)为 0.19%,检测率(RR)为 76.30%,根据公式(2-21)可得检测系统的可靠性为 99.81%。

被第一级分类器拒绝识别的样本是较难识别的样本,我们设计了第二级级联分类器对其进行进一步处理。第二级集成分类器的设计主要根据表 2.2 中的结果,表 2.2 中的结果表明大部分分类器对简单融合 HOG 和 Contourlet 特征并不能得到更好的识别效果,更好的解决方法是能够保存两种特征之间的相互关系。从上一节的分析中得出 MLP 能够通过对 HOG 和 Contourlet 特征进行非线性组合提取关键特征进而达到提升识别率的效果,另外基于神经网络对不同输入和网络结构能够体现多样性的考虑,我们在第二级级联分类器中使用 MLP 作为基分类器。

MLP 基分类器的训练数据是使用旋转森林方法经过对特征集进行随机分割、线性变换及构造稀疏矩阵得到,这里原始训练集是 HOG 和 Contourlet 特征的简单串联特征。分别使用变换后的 M_2 个训练集对 MLP 进行训练。在识别阶段,第二级集成分类器将对被第一级拒绝的样本进行识别。与第一级类似,第二级识别的最终结果采用 k/M_2 多数投票的方式决定,其中 k 为决定"拒识"率的阈值。最后系统的总识别率将根据第一级和第二级的识别结果综合得到。根据 Zhang[37] 对集成分类器个数的实验,我们设置 MLP 基分类器的个数为 $M_2=5$,当有 3 个基分类器结果达成一致时接受对样本的识别,否则依然拒绝对其的识别。通过对样本进行测试,将被第一级拒绝识别的 127 个样本使用第二级分类器进行识

别,第二级拒绝识别样本个数为 38 个,错误识别样本 9 个。则第二级系统识别率为 62.99%,误识率为 7.08%,"拒识"率为 29.92%,系统可靠性为 92.91%。根据之前的分析可知,系统"拒识"样本共有 38 个,误识样本共 10 个,系统的总识别率为 91.11%,总"拒识"率为 7.04%,总误识率为 1.85%,则可得系统的总的可靠性为 98.15%。

图 2-25　部分被"拒识"的样本,主要受 ROI 区域获取不当及光照影响

对比表 2.2 和表 2.3 的结果,在正确识别率上级联集成分类器比朴素贝叶斯、k-近邻及单个 MLP 分类器都高,SVM 的识别率虽然比较高,但 SVM 的误识率比级联集成分类器高,即可靠性比较低,这是由于输入样本比较模糊、受光照影响比较大或由于程序自动获取的车脸区域位置不完全造成的。在实际的识别系统中,如果对这些样本进行强分类,会对统计工作造成影响,而将比较难分的少数样本留给人工进行分类,则会降低误识带来的风险,如图 2-25 所示为本文所使用数据库中一些难分的样本,即被分类器拒绝识别的样本。

图中第一行显示的被拒绝识别样本主要是由于所截取的感兴趣区域位置包含背景区域造成的,第二行的样本主要受白天光照的影响,导致前脸区域上出现反光和边缘模糊现象,第三行显示的测试样本为傍晚时采集,此时光照强度不够,导致所采集的车辆图片信息比较模糊。分析图 2-25 所示的被拒绝识别的样本,本文所设计的模式识别系统放弃了对它们的识别,但这些样本可以由人工来完成识别,如果使用程序对他们进行强分,显然会得到不太理想的结果,进而可能在盗拍车辆检索过程中漏掉重要信息。

在级联集成分类器的第二级中,有 47 个车辆前脸样本(38 个被"拒识"+9 个误识)没有被系统正确识别。上一章提出的基于神经网络的旋转森林集成分类器有一种不带"拒识"选项的识别方式,即使用每个 MLP 预测输入测试样本属于每个类型的概率,将样本归属于对应的具有最大概率总和的类型。为了进一步探讨"拒识"和误识之间的关系,我们采用不带"拒识"功能的判别方式将 38 个被拒绝识别的样本进行硬分类,识别结果为:正确识别的样本数目为 17 个,错误识别的样本数目为 21 个。由于系统在第一级有一个误识的样本,则系统总误识样本数目为 21+9+1=31 个,此时系统的正确识别率为 94.26%,所有被误识的样本以及被识别成的类型如图 2-26 所示。

从图 2-26 可以看出,误识的样本多为光照条件及 ROI 区域中有背景干扰的样本,而通过设计有"拒识"选项的识别系统则可放弃对这些样本的识别,由人工对模糊样本处理会提高整个系统的可靠性。当我们使用带有"拒识"选项的系统方案进行识别时,总的误识率为 1.85%,当我们不使用"拒识"项时,总的误识率为 5.74%。

图 2-26 不具有"拒识"选项的识别系统的所有误识样本及误识目标类型

2.5 小结

为了解决交通监控系统中交通流量统计分析、假牌车辆识别和自动收费系统对不同车型进行自动计费等问题,本章研究了静态图像中车辆区域定位及车辆类型识别两种技术。

首先提出了一种基于对称特征融合的车辆检测方法,在规定当车辆包围框覆盖车辆90%以上区域且包围框尺寸与车辆尺寸相差不超过10%时为正确识别的情况下识别率为90.7%,与单纯基于轮廓特征、基于车牌、基于 Gabor 和 GLCM 特征及 SVM 的方法相比效果提升显著。其次,为了有效描述车脸图像,本文采用高可分辨性图像特征提升识别效果,例如 HOG 和 Contourlet 特征。同时为了避免维数灾难问题,文中提出了使用主成分分析(PCA)对特征进行降维。另外,为了探讨两种不同特征融合互补提高识别率的可能性,本文提出了将 HOG 和 Contourlet 两种特征的简单串联作为分类器的输入特征,并通过实验验证了该方法的可行性。

通过设计级联集成分类器方案在保证系统可靠性的同时提高了样本正确识别率。不单纯追求系统的高识别率,引入"拒识"选项降低了误识带来的风险。级联集成分类器是一个串行的方法,第二级的输入样本是第一级被拒绝的样本,可以通过引入多级级联分类器进一步降低被"拒识"的样本的数目。我们设计的级联分类器的第一级由 8 个不同的分类机制组成,第二级是使用 MLP 作为基分类器并结合旋转森林变换后的特征样本进行识别。两级集成分类器都具有拒绝识别不确定或模糊样本的功能。在平衡"拒识"样本数目和系统可靠性的关系后,我们得到了一个高可靠性并且高识别率的系统,最后系统的可靠性为98.15%,其中有 7.04%的样本被"拒识"。

关于车型识别,我们可以研究的内容还有很多。如前所述,模式识别系统需要解决两个重要的问题:①如何描述图像特征;②怎样使用所选取的特征识别图像。描述图像特征的方法有很多种,如本文提到的 HOG 和 Contourlet 特征,但不同的特征是从不同的角度阐述图像,研究如何使用多种特征的融合特征是一个比较热的话题,本文通过简单将两种特征串联在 MLP 中得到了较好的结果,但在其他分类器中识别效果确并不理想。目前有种比较有影响力的特征融合方法是 SVM 框架中的多核学习,它通过线性组合不同特征得到它们的核,并且这种方法能够从不同的源数据中提取特征,在接下来的研究工作中可以涉及这方面的内容。对于模式识别中的另外一个问题,即如何设计分类器进行特征训练和识别,本文介绍了两种分类器集成的方法,一种通过使用相同的特征输入而基分类器不同,另外一种是通过将特征集分割变换成不同的训练特征,并使用相同的 MLP 基分类器进行训练,MLP 对不同输入特征响应不稳定的特点使其成为集成分类器中一种较好的基分类器。分类器集成的方法还有很多种,比较著名的方法如前所述 Bagging,Boosting 等,其中 Boosting 方法在人脸检测上得到了卓越的效果,Boosting 的原理是通过筛选有效特征降分类误差控制在一个阈值范围内,并将筛选的特征作为弱分类器,输入测试样本的最终识别结果是每个弱分类器的加权输出,将这种方法扩展应用于车型分类应不失为一种较好的方法。

第三章
路面信息感知理论与技术

在国内外路面破损检测及识别研究成果的基础上,本文研究基于线阵CCD图像的路面破损自动检测及分类方法,主要研究有以下三个方面:

(1) 基于联合检测器的路面图像破损检测方法。由于路面图像中不可避免地存在噪声,而离散噪声引起的灰度突变与路面破损位置的灰度突变相似,因此如何有效地削弱背景噪声的影响,是图像破损检测的首要前提。路面破损检测是路面养护管理工作的决策依据,因此,确保路面破损的检测率是图像破损检测的重点。本文从路面破损图像灰度较正常路面灰度较暗这一特点出发,研究领域灰度差分法、灰度最小分析法和分块检测法三种路面破损检测方法,以构建一种高效的联合检测器用于路面图像的破损检测。

(2) 基于Contourlet变换的路面破损图像特征的提取方法。特征描述是实现路面破损自动化分类的基础,其关键是选择合适的特征描述子对路面破损进行特征描述。Contourlet变换是通过对路面破损图像进行多尺度分析,从而实现一种多分辨率、多方向和局域的图像特征表征,因此,本文研究基于Contourlet变换的路面破损图像特征提取方法,并与边缘方向直方图(Edge Orientation Histogram,EOH)、方向梯度直方图(Histogram of Orientation Gradients,HOG)和分层梯度方向直方图(Pyramid of Histogram of Orientation Gradients,PHOG)三种图像特征提取方法进行对比。

(3) 基于联合特征及分类器集成的路面破损图像分类方法。自动化识别分类是路面破损检测的最终目的,根据路面破损的特征描述,运用模式分类器对提取的特征进行机器学习和分类器训练,从而实现对路面破损图像的自动化识别分类。因此,本文研究基于随机子空间的支持向量机(Support Vector Machine,SVM)分类器集成的路面破损自动识别方法,并进行实验。

3.1 基于联合检测器的路面破损检测方法

路面破损状况评价是公路管理部门进行路面养护管理的重要依据,并在养护管理决策中占据重要地位,而路面破损检测是实现路面破损状况评价的前提。传统的路面破损检测方法存在着劳动强度大、工作效率低等缺点,为了更好地实施路面养护管理,公路管理部门迫切需要智能化的路面破损检测方法。因此,本章主要研究基于线阵CCD图像的路面破损自动检测方法,以实现对路面破损的高精度检测。

3.1.1 路面破损图像采集

本文采用自主研发的 DN-2011 型车载便携式公路路面病害检测设备采集路面破损图像,如图 3-1 所示,该设备由高精度 GPS 接收机提供的瞬时速度驱动高分辨率的线阵 CCD 相机,以实现对公路路面进行扫描获取高精度线阵图像。采集的路面图像的分辨率为 $2\,048 \times 1\,024$,如图 3-2 所示,图 3-2(a)~(d) 分别为横裂、纵裂、网裂和正常四种类型。从图 3-2 可以看出,对于路面破损图像,其裂缝位置的灰度值较正常位置的图像灰度值暗,且图像中含有阴影、砂砾等噪声,因此,图像处理算法应充分考虑到图像噪声的处理及细小破损的检测识别。

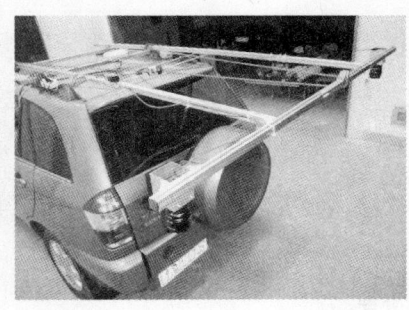
(a)

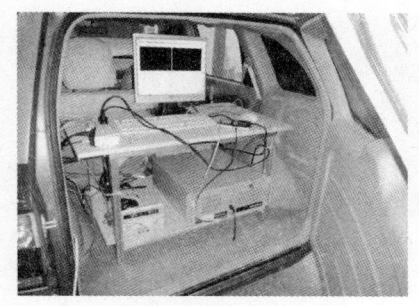
(b)

图 3-1 DN-2011 型车载便携式公路路面病害检测设备

(a) 横裂

(b) 纵裂

(c) 网裂

(d) 正常

图 3-2 路面破损线阵图像

3.1.2 图像预处理

路面破损图像易受道路环境及光照因素的影响,并且路面破损图像中往往存在砂砾、油污和阴影等噪声,干扰噪声的存在导致路面破损图像中的灰度及光照不均匀,严重影响了路面图像中破损信息的检测。因此,需要对路面图像进行预处理以消除图像中噪声信息,并对路面破损信息进行增强。

1) 道路标线信息去除

为保障车辆行驶的安全性,往往会在道路路面上添加道路标线对车辆驾驶进行引导。由于道路标线的存在,使得正常路面的背景相对道路标线而言灰度较暗,这将影响设备对破损信息的检测,因此在图像预处理中首先需要消除道路中的道路标线。对于路面图像中的道路标线而言,由于道路标线一般为白色或黄色,其灰度值与路面背景灰度存在较大的差异,因此通过对图像进行灰度约束即可去除路面中的道路标线信息。

　　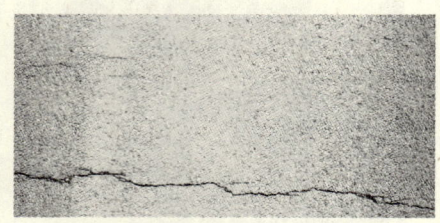

(a) 原始路面图像　　　　　　　　　　(b) 灰度处理后的路面图像

图 3-3　灰度处理

对于图 3-3(a)中的任意像素点 $I(i,j)$,有

$$I'(i,j) = \begin{cases} \mu & I(i,j) > \mu \\ I(i,j) & I(i,j) \leqslant \mu \end{cases} \quad (3\text{-}1)$$

其中,μ 为整幅图像的均值。通过式(3-1)约束可实现对图像中道路标线信息的去除,其处理效果如图 3-3(b)所示。

2) 图像阴影去除

路面破损图像易受道路两旁树木、栅栏和建筑物等遮挡影响而形成阴影,阴影的存在造成图像中阴影区域的像素灰度较暗,从而严重影响了路面图像中破损信息的检测。针对图像中阴影的去除,参考文献[109,110]采用人机交互的方法人工标定图像中的阴影区域,再对标定区域进行亮度的补偿;基于阴影区域的光谱不变性,Salvador 等[111]结合阴影区域的几何特征对阴影区域进行划分并进行亮度补偿。前者需要人工的干预,而后者对阴影的检测补偿主要是针对目标引起的阴影的去除,对于路面图像中由外部物体引起的阴影则无法消除。

由于图像阴影区域的灰度深度自区域中心向周围逐步缩减,本文采用基于亮度高程模型的图像阴影去除方法,以实现路面图像中阴影的去除[112]。基于亮度高程模型的图像阴影去除是基于地理地图中的等高线模型提出来的,由于图像中阴影的强度是由阴影中心向阴影边界逐渐递减的,因此模型将阴影强度按照强度的不同划分为不同的等级,然后再对各等级进行相应灰度补偿,实现阴影的去除。具体的方法如下:

(1) 对图像进行形态学闭运算。由于裂缝亮度与阴影区域的亮度较为接近,为了避免将裂缝划入阴影区内而执行亮度补偿,需要在阴影区域划分前将裂缝去除,因此采用灰度形态学闭运算对原始路面图像进行处理。

(2) 高斯平滑。对上述处理后的路面图像进行平滑处理,消除路面纹理对后续阴影区域划分的影响。

(3) 亮度等高区域划分。首先计算图像每一像素所应含有的平均像素数 ng,并计算图像各个灰度级所含有的像素数,按照灰度级大小对各级像素数进行求和相加,当像素数之和 $\geqslant ng$ 时,将当前所加像素对应的灰度级分为一个区域,依次对整幅图像的灰度级进行划分,最终图像分为 N 个区域。并根据经验阈值 $L = 7/8N$ 对图像进行区域划分,将图像分为阴影区域和非阴影区域。

(4) 具有纹理平衡的亮度补偿。对于非阴影区域 B 和阴影区域 S,分别按照式(3-2)对该区域像素进行变换,实现亮度的补偿,即

$$I'_{i,j} = \begin{cases} \alpha \cdot I_{i,j} + \lambda & \text{if } (i,j) \in S \\ I_{i,j} & \text{if } (i,j) \in B \end{cases} \tag{3-2}$$

其中,$\alpha = \dfrac{D_B}{D_S}$,$D_B$、$D_S$ 分别为非阴影区和阴影区的像素亮度值的标准方差,$\lambda = \hat{I}_B - \alpha \cdot \hat{I}_S$,$\hat{I}_B$、$\hat{I}_S$ 分别为非阴影区和阴影区的平均亮度。

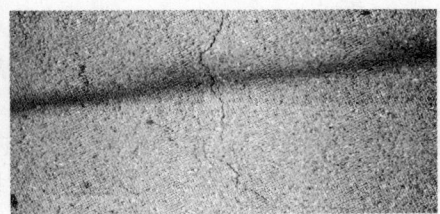
(a) 原始含阴影路面图像

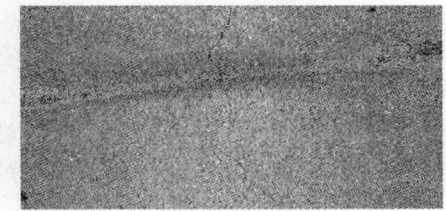
(b) 阴影去除后路面图像

图 3-4　高程模型阴影去除

采用高程模型消除图 3-4(a)阴影的结果如图 3-4(b)所示,路面图像中阴影得以去除。但是,在消除阴影的同时也削弱了路面图像的破损目标,主要原因是原始路面图像光线较暗,阴影的灰度特性与路面图像中破损的灰度特性过于相似,从而导致在对阴影区域的灰度增强的同时也对破损的灰度进行了增强。

3) 图像频域滤波处理

路面图像中的噪声主要是沥青路面不平整性及路面砂砾的离散性造成的,此类噪声信息的纹理特性与路面图像的纹理特性类似,因此,仅从纹理特性对路面破损图像进行降噪处理容易造成路面图像中破损目标信息的缺失。图像去噪的关键是在去除噪声的同时能完整保留图像的原有细节信息,小波阈值去噪是由 Donoho 等[113]提出来的,该方法的特点是方法简单和计算量较小,近来在图像去噪领域得到了广泛的应用。对于路面破损图像而言,图像中的破损信息较少而背景信息较多,这恰恰符合小波阈值去噪的特性,因此,本文采用小波阈值去噪的方法来消除路面破损图像中的噪声。

在小波阈值去噪中,对于经小波变换后的图像,包含有信号重要信息的小波系数其幅值较大,但数量较少,而噪声对应的小波系数幅值小,则通过选取适当的阈值,将小于阈值的小

波系数置零,保留大于阈值的小波系数,从而抑制信号中的噪声。对于小波阈值去噪,主要有以下步骤:

(1) 对噪声图像 $\{I_{ij}, i, i=1, 2, \cdots, N\}$ 做小波变换,得到小波系数 $\{W_{ij}, i, i=1, 2, \cdots, N\}$;

(2) 对上步得到的小波系数 W_{ij} 进行阈值处理, $\overline{W_{ij}} = \eta_T(W_{ij})$, $i, j = 1, 2, \cdots, N$, 其中, $\eta_T(\cdot)$ 为阈值函数,T 为选取的阈值;

(3) 对小波去噪处理后的小波系数 $\overline{W_{ij}}$ 进行小波逆变换,得到去噪后的图像。

由上述步骤可知,小波阈值去噪的关键是阈值函数及阈值的选择。常见的阈值函数可以分为硬阈值函数、软阈值函数和半软阈值函数,它们的基本思想都是认为代表图像中噪声信息的小波系数较小,应将其去除,而对较大的小波系数进行保留。对于本文的路面图像去噪,由于图像尺寸较大,考虑到图像预处理耗费的时间及对后续破损检测的影响,本文选取小波阈值去噪函数中的硬阈值去噪,而其阈值选用通用 Visushrink 阈值,以期在实现图像去噪的同时不增加图像处理算法的复杂度,提高处理算法的效率。硬阈值函数表达为

$$\eta_T(w_{ij}) = \begin{cases} 0 & |w_{ij}| \leqslant T \\ w_{ij} & |w_{ij}| > T \end{cases} \tag{3-3}$$

其中,选取阈值 $T = \sigma_n\sqrt{2\log(N)}$。采用小波硬阈值函数及 Visushrink 阈值对图 3-5(a)进行去噪处理,处理结果如图 3-5(b)所示。小波去噪处理后的路面图像较原始图像而言,其路面破损背景部分由于沥青路面不平整性造成的毛刺噪声得到了有效的削弱,图像中离散的白色噪声点也得以去除,且实现了在去除噪声的同时较为完整地保留了图像中的目标破损信息。

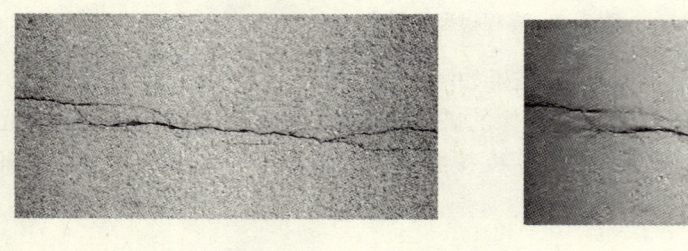

(a)   (b)

图 3-5 小波硬阈值函数及 Visushrink 阈值去噪

3.1.3 基于灰度分析的路面破损检测

在数字图像处理领域,图像的灰度即图像的深度。路面破损图像的显著特点是路面破损位置的图像比正常路面位置的深度暗,即路面破损位置的像素灰度比正常路面像素灰度值小,基于这一事实,本文开展基于灰度分析的路面破损检测方法研究。

1) 领域灰度差分法

传统阈值分割是通过对图像设定阈值将图像像素分为若干类,其考虑的是图像的全局灰度特征,往往忽略图像的局部细节信息,领域灰度差分法是对传统阈值分割的改进。领域灰度差分法是利用图像的局部灰度特征,通过对像素点周边领域像素灰度值与中心像素的灰度差分确定中心像素的灰度特征,其优点是充分考虑了图像的局部细节特征,且能够削弱图像中离散噪声的影响。

对于路面灰度图像中任意一像素点,其灰度值为 $p(x, y)$,其整幅图像的像素灰度级为 $val([1, 2, \cdots, L])$,则对于该点像素周边 W 领域内像素,其灰度差分值为 $a_{val, p(x, y)}$,即

$$a_{val, p(x, y)} = \sum_{j=1}^{W}[p_j - p(x, y)] \tag{3-4}$$

对于灰度值为 val 的像素点 $p(x, y)$,$a_{val, p(x, y)}$ 反映了其 W 领域内各像素点与该中心像素的灰度差分。$a_{val, p(x, y)}$ 值表征在该像素点位置的灰度梯度值的大小,能有效地反映图像中的灰度梯度变化。对于一张图像而言,其灰度值的变化范围为 $[1, 2, \cdots, L]$,则对于每一灰度级 val,统计图像中具有相同灰度值 val 的差分值 A_{val},即

$$A_{val} = \iint a_{val, p(x, y)} \mathrm{d}x \mathrm{d}y \tag{3-5}$$

则对于大小为 $X \times Y$ 的图像,$x \in [1, 2, \cdots, X]$,$y \in [1, 2, \cdots, Y]$,则 A_{val} 为

$$A_{val} = \sum_{x=1}^{X}\sum_{y=1}^{Y} a_{val, p(x, y)} \tag{3-6}$$

由于路面破损图像中破损位置灰度较正常路面灰度较低,因此,破损位置像素灰度与其领域像素灰度差分值较大。对于一幅图像取其最大差分值 A_{val} 的灰度级 val 代表的就是破损位置的像素灰度,因此,领域灰度差分的阈值选取规则为

$$t = \mathrm{Max}_{i=1}^{L} A_i \tag{3-7}$$

利用灰度阈值 t 将路面破损图像中的裂缝区域与背景区域进行分割,即

$$p(x, y) = \begin{cases} 1 & p(x, y) \leqslant t \\ 0 & p(x, y) > t \end{cases} \tag{3-8}$$

采用领域灰度差分法对经过预处理后的图 3-2(a)~(d)进行破损区域检测,检测结果如图 3-6(a)~(d)所示。由检测结果分析可知,领域灰度差分法对图像光照因素的影响不敏感,对于亮度较暗的图像仍能取得较好的检测结果,具有一定的鲁棒性,但该算法对网裂破损及细微破损的检测效果较差,主要是因为网裂和细微破损的领域灰度梯度效果不明显。

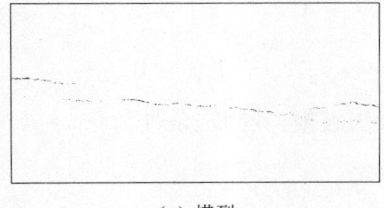

(a) 横裂

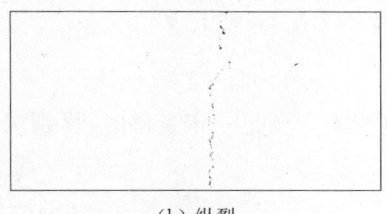

(b) 纵裂

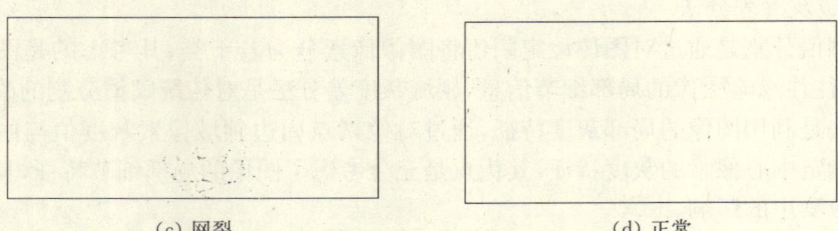

图 3-6 领域差分法检测结果

2) 局部灰度最小分析法

路面破损图像通常存在砂砾和阴影,从而导致并不是所有灰度值较周围小的像素点是裂缝点,局部灰度最小分析法可以在利用路面破损的灰度特征的同时,同时兼顾考虑裂缝的局部联通性。局部灰度最小分析法通过对图像中像素进行遍历搜索,获取图像各行各列的最小灰度像素,并据此对图像中各像素点进行判定。其判定原则为:对于大小为 $M \times N$ 的图像 I 中的任意像素点 $I(x, y)$,如果该点像素灰度为像素所在行(列)中为灰度最小值,则标记该像素点行(列)标记为 1,否则标记为 0,即

$$\left. \begin{array}{l} L_x[x, y] = \begin{cases} 1 & \forall_{j \in \{1, 2, \cdots, N\}} : I[x, y] = \min\{I[x, j] \mid x \in \{1, 2, \cdots, M\}\} \\ 0 & \text{otherwise} \end{cases} \\ L_y[x, y] = \begin{cases} 1 & \forall_{j \in \{1, 2, \cdots, M\}} : I[x, y] = \min\{I[j, y] \mid y \in \{1, 2, \cdots, N\}\} \\ 0 & \text{otherwise} \end{cases} \end{array} \right\} \tag{3-9}$$

则对于图像 I 中各像素点的行标记和列标记矩阵 L_x 和 L_y,对 L_x 和 L_y 进行求和得到矩阵 $L[x, y]$,即

$$L[x, y] = L_x[x, y] + L_y[x, y] \tag{3-10}$$

则对于 $L:\{1, 2, \cdots, M\} \times \{1, 2, \cdots, N\}$ 其取值为 $\{0, 1, 2\}$。当 $L[x, y] = 0$ 代表该像素点 $I(x, y)$ 不是局部最小值像素点;当 $L[x, y] = 1$ 代表像素点 $I(x, y)$ 仅在水平或垂直方向是最小值点;当 $L[x, y] = 2$ 代表像素点 $I(x, y)$ 在水平和垂直方向均为最小像素点;在矩阵 $L[x, y]$ 中,其非零元素的个数最大为 $N+M$,最小为 $\sqrt{N^2 + M^2}$。对于标记的矩阵 $L[x, y]$,其非零元素对应的图像像素灰度为局部灰度最小像素,但由于在路面图像中存在砂砾、阴影等噪声,导致所有标记的灰度最小值点并不都是破损像素,因此需要对标记点做进一步的标定确认,其判定过程如下:

(1) 选取 $L[x, y]$ 中两非零元素对应的像素点 $L[x_1, y_1]$、$L[x_2, y_2]$,则由两像素点可确定一条直线 $l_{1,2}$,对于 $\forall_{x \in (x_1, x_2), y \in (y_1, y_2)}$ 有

$$l_{1,2} : (y - y_1)(x_2 - x_1) - (y_2 - y_1)(x - x_1) = 0 \tag{3-11}$$

(2) 则当 $l_{1,2}$ 满足一定条件时,可判定该直线为破损,其判定条件为

$$M_e \geqslant \frac{1}{l_{1,2}(S)} \sum_{a, b \in S} (I[a, b] - M_e) - \tau \tag{3-12}$$

其中，$M_e = \text{mean}(I[x_1, y_1], I[x_2, y_2])$，$S$ 为直线 $l_{1,2}$ 上所有点的集合。

（3）相对于图像中噪声像素的离散特性，路面破损图像中路面破损往往具有局部连通性，因此，为了缩减算法的计算量，定义两备选像素点之间的距离应满足如下条件

$$d = \sqrt{(x_2-x_1)^2 + (y_2-y_1)^2} < r \tag{3-13}$$

其中，r 为设定的距离阈值。

（4）对于同时满足上述两条件的直线 $l_{1,2}$ 上的像素点，令其对应二值化图像的像素值为 1，否则为 0，则经过判定，可获取到图像对应的二值化图像，实现对图像中路面破损的检测。

采用局部灰度最小分析法对经过预处理后的图 3-2(a)～(d)进行破损区域检测，检测结果如图 3-7(a)～(d)所示。由检测结果分析可知，局部灰度最小分析法可有效地检测路面破损图像中细小裂缝，但对网裂破损的检测效果不明显，并且该方法检测结果中含有较多的噪声信息，且检测到的二值化目标像素较为离散。

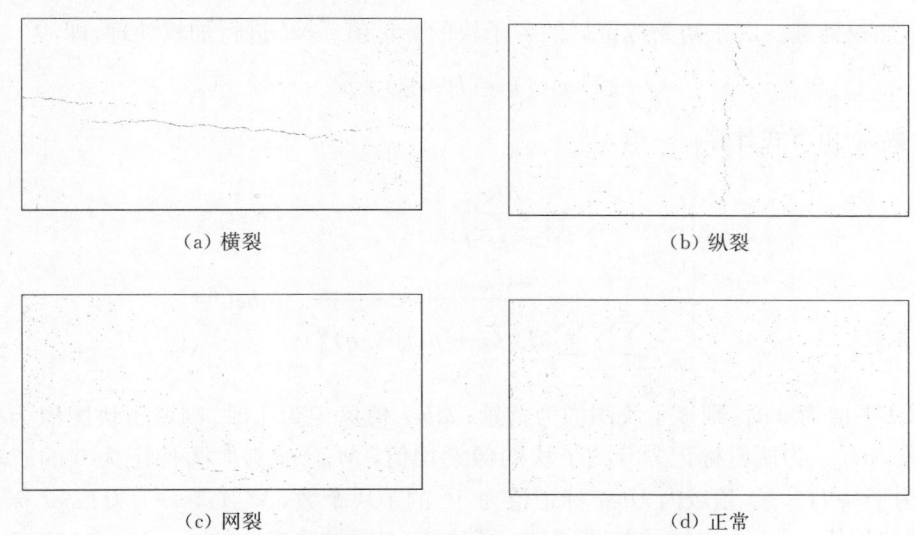

(a) 横裂　　　　　　　　　　　　(b) 纵裂

(c) 网裂　　　　　　　　　　　　(d) 正常

图 3-7　局部灰度最小分析法检测结果

3) 分块标记法

通常路面破损图像中的破损像素所占整幅图像的像素比例较小，而图像中绝大部分信息是背景信息，因此，可以将路面破损图像进行分块检测，统计各子块图像的特征，进而再对图像各子块进行细分处理。对于输入大小为 $M \times N$ 的图像，网格化为 $W \times L$ 的子块，其子块的大小选择应考虑原图大小及待检测目标的大小，子块太小容易导致错误的裂缝检测，太大则易丢失微裂缝。本文中原始图像大小为 2 048×1 024，构建的子块大小为 128×64，则图像被分为 16×16 个子块。对分割后的各子块图像建立均值特征矩阵 M_m 和方差特征矩阵 Std_m 两个特征矩阵，分块标记法的具体步骤如下：

（1）初始标记。本文采用初始标记法来区分路面破损图像中背景和目标，以实现针对性的图像增强。图像的初始标记的原则为对于每一子块 (i, j)，根据子块的特征矩阵，建立

子块标记的标记原则，即

$$label^{(i,j)} = lable_H^{(i,j)} \vee lable_V^{(i,j)} \tag{3-14}$$

$$\left.\begin{array}{l} lable_H^{(i,j)} = [std(Ah^{(i,j)}) > (k_1 \times std(Bh^i) + k_2 \times mean(Bh^i))] \\ \qquad \wedge [(Ah^{(i,j)}[1] - Ah^{(i,j)}[2]) > 0] \\ lable_V^{(i,j)} = [std(Av^{(i,j)}) > (k_1 \times std(Bv^j) + k_2 \times mean(Bv^j))] \\ \qquad \wedge [(Av^{(i,j)}[1] - Av^{(i,j)}[2]) > 0] \end{array}\right\} \tag{3-15}$$

其中，$Ah^{(i,j)} = \left[\dfrac{M_m(i,j-1) + M_m(i,j+1)}{2}; M_m(i,j)\right]$，$Bh^i = [0; std(Ah^{(i,2)}), \cdots,$ $std(Ah^{(i,15)};0)]$，$Av^{(i,j)} = \left[\dfrac{M_m(i-1,j) + M_m(i+1,j)}{2}; M_m(i,j)\right]^T$，$Bv^j = [0;$ $std(Av^{(2,j)}), \cdots, std(Ah^{(i,15)};0)]^T$，参数 k_1 和 k_2 的取值采用线性规划在人为监督的情况下获取。

（2）加权处理。对于初始标记后的各子块的标记值 label 进行加权处理，即

$$I'(i,j) = I(i,j) * nc \tag{3-16}$$

其中，参数 nc 由下式计算：

$$nc = \begin{cases} \dfrac{val_{back}}{M_m(i,j)^{'0'}} & label = 0 \\ \dfrac{val_{back}}{\dfrac{1}{k^{'0'}} \sum_{p=-a}^{a} \sum_{q=-b}^{b} M_m(i+p, j+q)^{'0'}} & label = 1 \end{cases} \tag{3-17}$$

当 label 值为 0 时，则该子块图像为背景；label 值标记为 1 时，则该子块图像为破损区域。参数 val_{back} 为所有标记为 0 的子块的像素均值，$M_m(i,j)^{'0'}$ 为标记为 0 的子块的均值，$k^{'0'}$ 为子块 $I(i,j)$ 领域内 label 标记值为 '0' 的子块个数，$M_m(i,j)^{'0'}$ 为 label 标记值为 0 的子块的均值，a、b 为领域的范围，例如：子块 3×3 领域内对应的 $a=b=1$，5×5 对应的 $a=b=2$。

（3）目标检测。对于存在破损的路面图像，其背景部分子块图像的均值较破损子块图像的均值较大，并且其方差反而较小，因此，可利用不同子块特征的差异对图像子块特征矩阵进行聚类分析，以实现对图像中目标（破损）子块的检测，本文采用无监督学习的 K 均值聚类算法进行路面破损检测。

K 均值聚类算法的主要思想是通过迭代把数据集划分成不同的类别，例如：对于路面图像 $I(i,j)$，计算图像各子块的均值特征和方差特征以构建特征矩阵，通过对图像特征的 K 均值聚类，将图像各子块分成 K 类以实现路面图像中破损区域检测。本文中取 K=2，采用分块标记法对 3-2(a)~(d) 进行破损区域检测，检测结果分别如图 3-8(a)~(d) 所示。由图 3-8 分析可得分块标记法对网裂的检测效果较好，且算法的处理速度较快，但易受图像中阴影的影响。

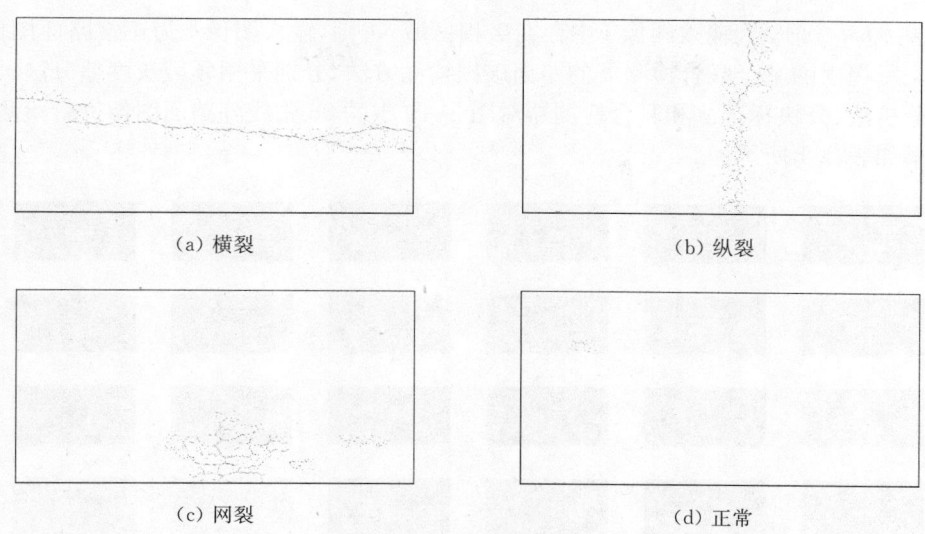

图 3-8 分块标记法检测结果

4）基于联合检测器的路面破损检测

由本节1）所述的理论及实验分析可得：领域灰度差分法对图像光照因素的影响不敏感，对于亮度较暗的图像仍能取得较好的检测结果；局部灰度最小分析法对路面破损图像中细小裂缝具有较好的检测效果，但对网裂破损的检测不明显；分块标记法对网裂具有较好检测效果，且算法的处理速度较快。上述三种路面破损检测方法各具有不同的优势和缺点，本文基于级联分类器的思想，采用领域灰度差分法、局部灰度最小分析法和分块标记法构建一种路面破损联合检测器用于提高路面破损检测率。

基于联合检测器的路面破损检测方法的流程图如图3-9所示，即

(1) 对于输入图像 I 采用领域灰度差分法进行破损检测，检测结果为 $label_1$，如果检测到路面破损，则 $label_1 = 1$，否则，$label_1 = 0$；

(2) 对于输入图像 I 采用局部灰度最小分析法进行破损检测，检测结果为 $label_2$，如果检测到路面破损，则 $label_2 = 1$，否则，$label_2 = 0$；

(3) 对于输入图像 I 采用分块标记法进行破损检测，检测结果为 $label_3$，如果检测到路面破损，则 $label_3 = 1$，否则，$label_3 = 0$；

(4) 计算上述三种方法对输入图像 I 的检测结果 $label$，即

$$label = \sum_{i=1}^{3} label_i \quad (3-18)$$

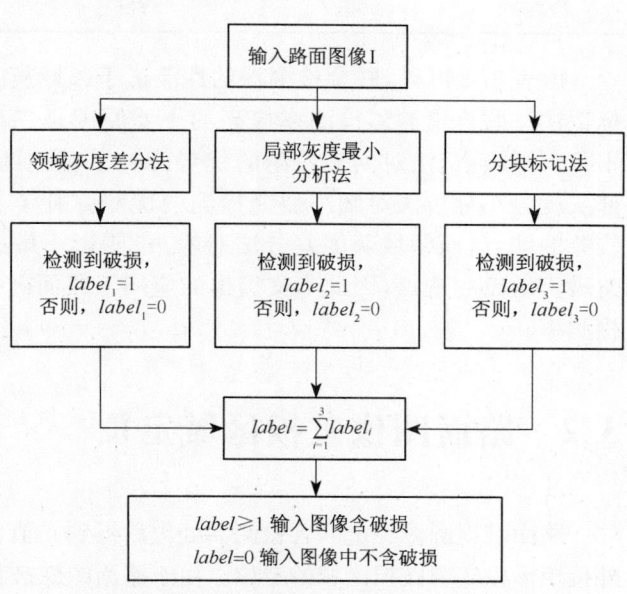

图 3-9 基于联合检测器的路面破损检测流程图

如果 $label \geqslant 1$，则输入图像 I 中存在破损区域，否则，输入图像 I 为正常路面图像。为验证本文所提出的基于联合检测器的路面破损检测方法，分别采用领域灰度差分法、局部灰度最小分析法、分块标记法和联合检测器对图 3-10 中的 36 张线阵路面图像进行检测处理，检测结果如表 3.1 所示。

图 3-10　实验图像

表 3.1　检测结果统计

检测方法	领域灰度差分法	局部灰度最小分析法	分块标记法	联合检测器
检测率	80%	60%	83.3%	96.7%

由表 3.1 可得，联合检测器的性能优于领域灰度差分法、局部灰度最小分析法和分块标记法。联合检测器检测率提高的主要原因是三种检测方法的联合较好弥补了各自的不足，分块标记法对网裂检测的优势弥补了其他两种方法在网裂检测方面的不足，而局部灰度最小分析法对细小裂缝检测的优势弥补了其他两种方法对细小破损的检测效果较差的缺点，而领域灰度差分法对噪声、阴影不敏感的优势也较好弥补了其他两种方法对噪声敏感的缺点，因此本文提出的应用于路面破损图像检测的联合检测器具有较高的检测率。

3.2　路面图像破损区域定位

路面破损图像经过联合检测器处理后得到二值化图像，计算二值化图像目标连通域的外接矩形以实现破损区域的定位。由于路面图像破损裂缝的分散性，需要对破损图像的连通区域进行合并，路面图像破损区域定位的具体方法如下：

(1) 连通区域标记。对于二值图像 $I_{ij}(i=0,1,2,\cdots,M,j=0,1,2,\cdots,N)$，计算二值图像中目标像素的连通度，并构建连通区域，计算并标记各连通区域的质心位置 $Q_{ij}(i,j)$。

(2) 连通区域融合。由于路面破损图像中裂缝的分散性造成二值化图像目标的整体连通性较差，需要对各连通区域进行融合，其连通区域融合过程如图 3-11 所示。

图 3-11　连通区域融合过程

首先计算各连通区域的质心位置，当两连通区域位置小于限定的距离长度时，将两连通区域进行融合。对于任意两连通区域质心位置 $Q_1(x_1,y_1)$、$Q_2(x_2,y_2)$，其质心距离 d 为

$$d=\sqrt{(x_2-x_1)^2+(y_2-y_1)^2} \tag{3-19}$$

设定允许融合的阈值 T，当两质心间距离满足 $d<T$ 时，对两连通区域进行融合，构建新的连通区域；反之，则对两连通区域不做融合处理，保持连通区域的独立性。

(3) 目标定位。根据连通区域的外接边界进行路面破损图像区域的精确定位。

对图 3-2(a)~(c)采用联合检测器进行破损检测，根据上述步骤进行目标定位，定位的结果如图 3-12 所示。

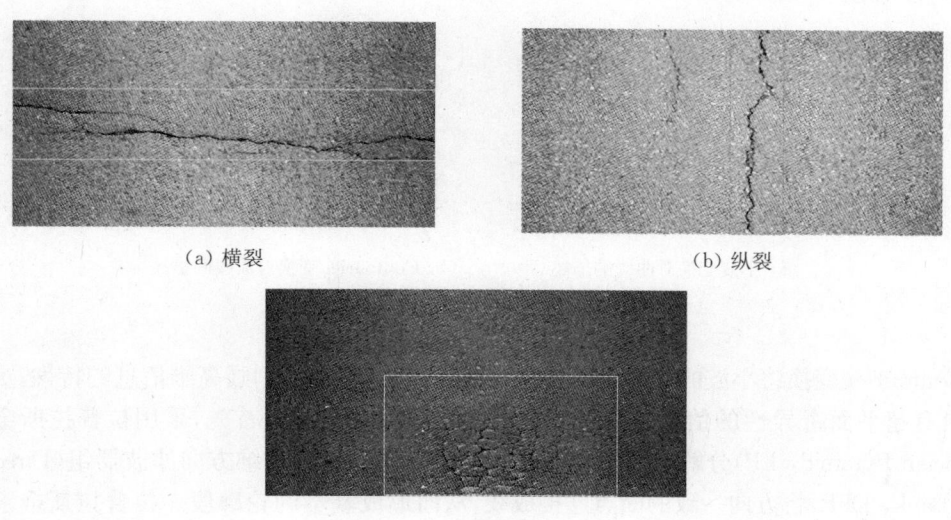

(a) 横裂　　　　　　　　　　　　　(b) 纵裂

(c) 网裂

图 3-12　路面破损定位结果

3.3　基于 Contourlet 变换的路面图像特征提取方法

为实现路面破损类型的自动化识别，需要研究路面破损图像的特征提取方法，特征提取

方法优良程度的判别标准主要有：所提取的图像特征能否有效地表征目标图像，使得分类的错误率降低；提取的图像特征应具有较低的维数；提取的图像特征应对噪声和不相关的图像转换不敏感。因为路面破损图像具有丰富的边缘纹理特征，即其灰度纹理特征显著，因此，本文研究基于 Contourlet 变换（Contourlet Transform，CT）的路面破损图像特征提取方法，并与边缘方向直方图（Edge Orientation Histogram，EOH）、方向梯度直方图（Histogram of Orientation Gradients，HOG）和分层梯度方向直方图（Pyramid of Histogram of Orientation Gradients，PHOG）三种特征提取方法进行对比分析，最后，采用支持向量机（Support Vector Machines，SVMs）分类器进行路面破损类型识别实验。

3.3.1 Contourlet 变换

Contourlet 变换是由 Do 等[114]提出的一种多尺度几何分析工具，具有良好的多分辨率、局部化和方向性等优良特性。与 Wavelet 变换相比，Contourlet 变换采用类似于轮廓段（Contour Segment）的基结构来逼近曲线，可在高频上做任意多个方向的分解，并提供各个方向的细节信息。Contourlet 变换基函数的支撑区间具有随尺度变化长宽比的"长条形"结构，具有方向性和各向异性，而二维小波是由一维小波张量积构建得到，只能限于用正方形支撑区间描述轮廓，不同大小的正方形对应小波的多分辨率结构，因而缺乏方向性且不具有各向异性，如图 3-13 所示。

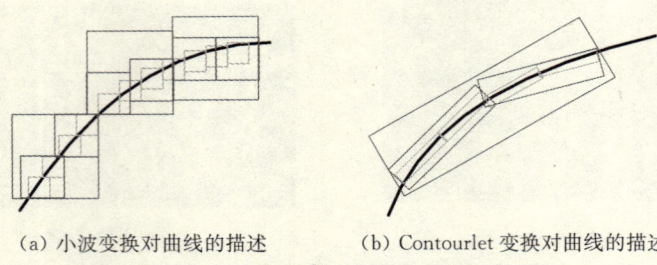

(a) 小波变换对曲线的描述　　(b) Contourlet 变换对曲线的描述

图 3-13　对曲线的描述的形式

Contourlet 变换将小波的优点延伸到高维空间，能够更好地刻画高维信息的特性，更适合处理具有超平面奇异性的信息。Contourlet 变换的基本思想是：首先，采用拉普拉斯金字塔（Laplacian Pyramid，LP）分解得到边缘的孤立断点，然后，使用二维方向滤波器组（Directional Filter Bank，DFB）将方向一致的断点连接成线，从而形成基本的轮廓段。拉普拉斯金字塔分解与重构如图 3-14 所示，H 和 G 分别为分解和合成滤波，M 为采样矩阵。经过拉普拉斯分

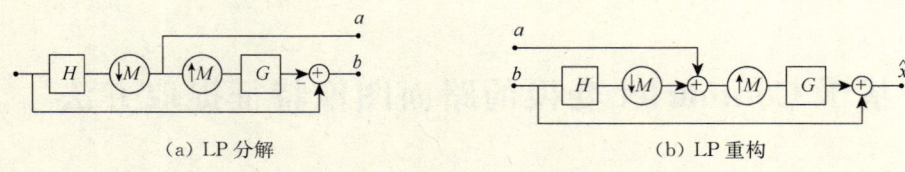

(a) LP 分解　　(b) LP 重构

图 3-14　拉普拉斯分解和重构

解的下采样图像为图像的低频信息 a,而下采样图像与预测图像的差图像为图像的高频信息 b。这种处理可以将下采样的低通信号 b 循环进行下去,最后形成第 n 层低通部分和 N 个细节部分(高频部分)组成的金字塔式的图像分解。

方向滤波器(DFB)是对图像的多方向性分析,即通过一个 l 层的二叉树分解,将输入图像分解成 2^l 个子带。经 LP 分解的高频信息经过 DFB 的处理可逐渐地将点奇异连成线结构,从而形成图像的轮廓。DFB 包括两通道的梅花滤波器组和平移操作两个模块,梅花滤波器组(Quincunx 滤波器,如图 3-15 所示)是用扇形滤波器将 2-D 光谱分成垂直和

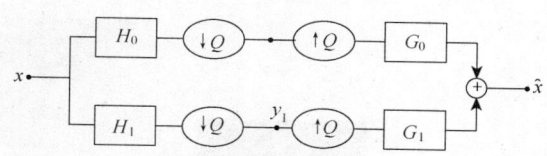

图 3-15 Quincunx 滤波器

水平两个方向。H 和 G 分别为分解和合成滤波器;Q 为采样矩阵,$Q_0 = \begin{pmatrix} 1 & -1 \\ 1 & 1 \end{pmatrix}$ 和 $Q_1 = \begin{pmatrix} 1 & 1 \\ -1 & 1 \end{pmatrix}$ 的不同在于图像反转的角度不同,分别为 45°和 −45°。

平移操作(Shearing)是在 Quincunx 滤波分解阶段之前进行,其作用是重新排序图像的采样。实施平移操作后图像被旋转并且宽度变为原来的两倍,在合成阶段再进行一个反 Shearing 操作对图像进行合成,Shearing 操作可采用 $R_0 = \begin{pmatrix} 1 & 1 \\ 0 & 1 \end{pmatrix}$、$R_1 = \begin{pmatrix} 1 & -1 \\ 0 & 1 \end{pmatrix}$、$R_2 = \begin{pmatrix} 1 & 0 \\ 1 & 1 \end{pmatrix}$ 和 $R_3 = \begin{pmatrix} 1 & 0 \\ -1 & 1 \end{pmatrix}$ 四种采样矩阵。实际上,DFB 的分解过程可以等效为如图 3-16 所示的并行结构,即每个方向子带是由图像通过对应的方向滤波器 E 后,再进行下采样 S 而得到的,右半部分为其对应的合成部分。对于多通道滤波器组 E,具有下列对角形式:

$$S_k^l = \begin{cases} \text{diag}(2^{l-1}, 2) & \text{for } 0 \leqslant k < 2^{l-1} \\ \text{diag}(2, 2^{l-1}) & \text{for } 2^{l-1} \leqslant k < 2^l \end{cases} \tag{3-20}$$

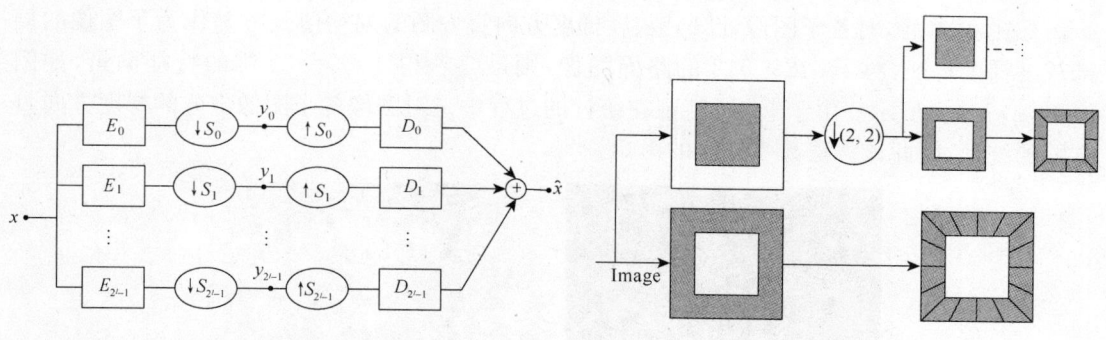

图 3-16 DFB 分解过程　　　　　图 3-17 Contourlet 变换过程

Contourlet 变换将金字塔分解和方向滤波器结合起来,弥补了金字塔分解不具有方向性和方向滤波器对低频分解性能差的弱点,其变换过程如图 3-17 所示。

对图 3-18(a)图像进行三层 Contourlet 分解,其中第 l 层分解的方向子带数为 2^l,最细

致层上的方向子带数为 16,其各层子带图像如图 3-18(b)所示。对于每一个细节矩阵,计算各矩阵的列均值及矩阵方差作为各层细节矩阵的特征,则图像的特征可由各细节矩阵的特征组合构成,则对于输入的 512×512 的路面图像,经过 Contourlet 特征提取后,获得图像的特征向量为 1×2 318 维。

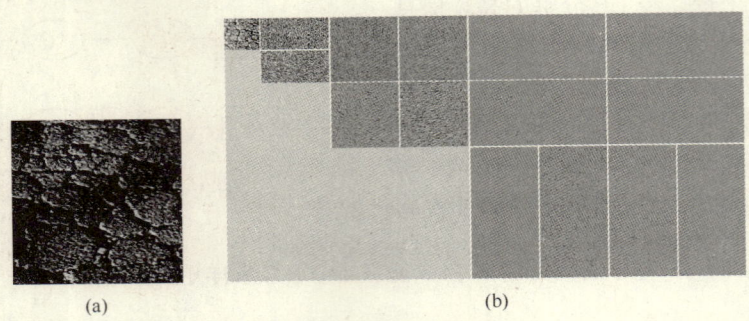

图 3-18 路面破损图像的三层 Contourlet 分解

3.3.2 其他纹理特征提取方法

1) 边缘方向直方图

边缘方向直方图(Edge Orientation Histogram,EOH)特征是对图像边缘信息及梯度信息的综合描述,其基本思想是图像的局部形状特征可以由局部灰度梯度和边缘方向来表征。首先,将一幅图像划分为多个子图像,并按照水平边缘方向、垂直边缘方向、对角边缘方向(包括两个斜对角)和无边缘方向 5 个方向对各子图像的梯度直方图进行分类;然后,对各梯度直方图按照划分的分类方向进行统计,得到的直方图特征即是图像的边缘方向直方图特征。

对于图 3-19(a)~(d)路面破损图像,首先,对图像进行边缘处理,并将边缘图像划分为 4 个子图像;然后,对各子图像计算其灰度梯度方向直方图的列均值及方差作为子图像的局部灰度梯度特征,对于 512×512 的路面图像,则最终获得 4×5=20 维的特征向量,如图 3-20(a)~(d)所示。由于 EOH 特征在统计的过程中是对图像各子图像部分的梯度方向直方图的统计,因此该方法易受噪声的影响。

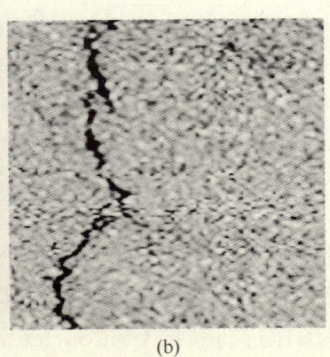

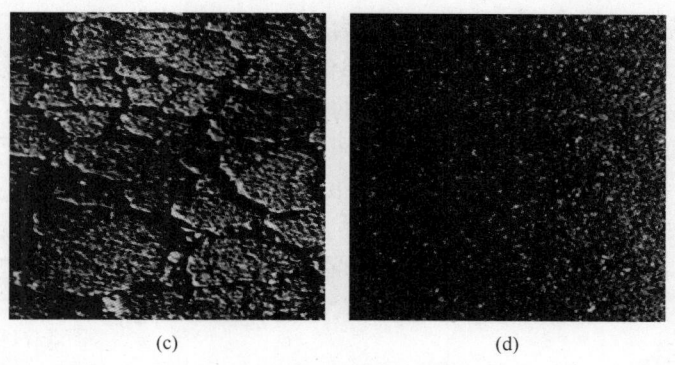

图 3-19 路面破损图像

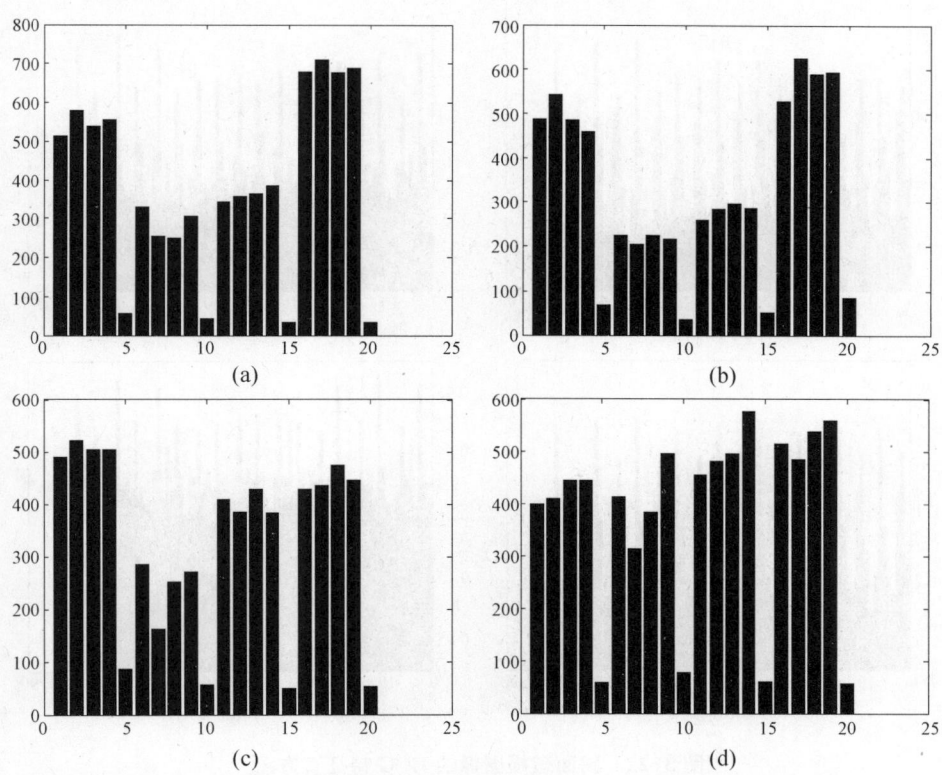

图 3-20 EOH 特征表征

2）梯度方向直方图

梯度方向直方图（Histogram of Orientation Gradients，HOG）特征[116]的主要思想是在梯度（或边缘）的确切位置不确定的情况下，利用图像的局部梯度（或边缘）方向的分布能够实现对图像中对象的局部外观和外形的描述。首先，将图像划分为小的单元格（cell），并在各单元格内进行统计该单元格子图像的一维梯度方向直方图；然后，将所有单元格的直方图统计结果连接起来，继而形成整个图像的 HOG 特征表示。对于图 3-21 中 512×512 的路面图像，首先，设置其细胞单元大小为 256×256，并在每个细胞单元内统计 9 个直方图通道的无向梯度(即将 0~180°的梯度方向划分为 9 个区间);然后,设置归一化块(block)的大小为 256×256(即各细胞单元作为独立的一个块),块在水平和竖直方向的步进大小均为 128;最后将所有细胞单元的直方图组合起来形成 HOG 特征描述子,得到的特征描述子大小为 9×3×3=81 维,各尺寸之间的相对关系如图 3-21 所示。

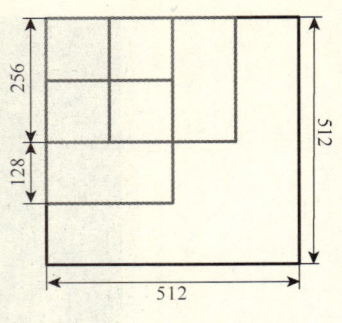

图 3-21 HOG 特征参数

对于图 3-19 中的路面破损图像进行 HOG 特征提取,动块的大小与胞元大小相同,移动步长为 128,结果分别如图 3-22(a)~(d)所示。

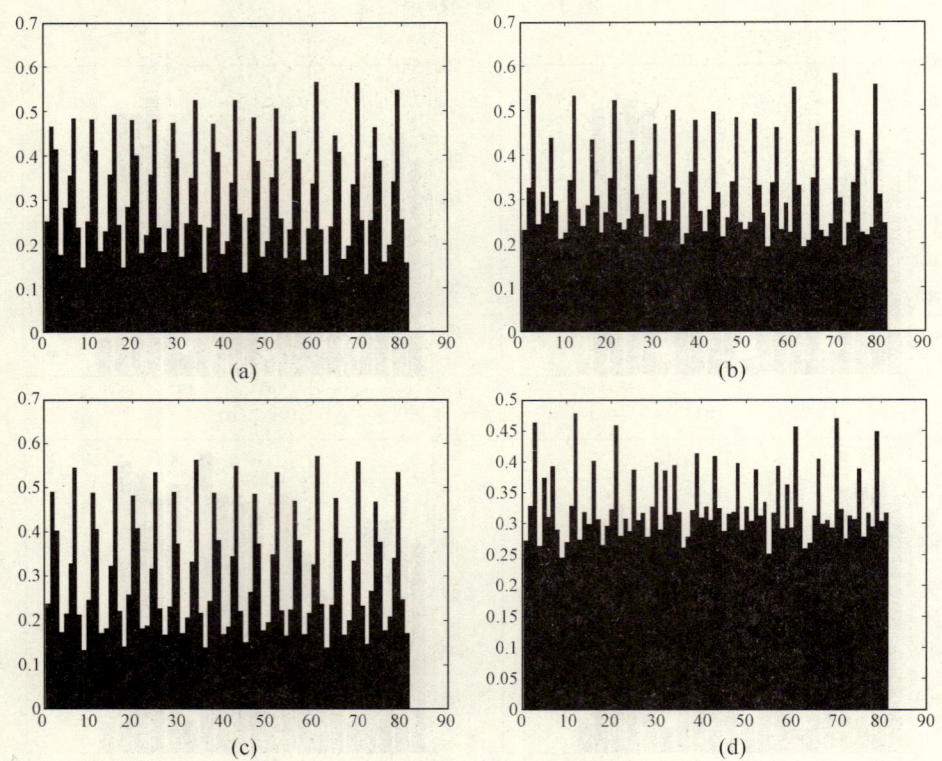

图 3-22 路面破损图像的 HOG 特征直方图

3) 分层梯度方向直方图

分层梯度方向直方图(Pyramid of Histogram of Orientation Gradients,PHOG)特征[117,118]是一种采用金字塔结构的梯度方向直方图描述特征的方法,该方法是通过使用空间四叉树分解形成图像的多分辨率表示,并联结从低分辨率到高分辨率的多级梯度方向直方图来描述图像,过程如图 3-23 所示。首先,提取输入的图像的边缘轮廓;然后将图像的边缘轮廓进行分层,每一层将上一层的各块按宽和高等分成更小的分块,分别提取各分块轮廓点的梯度方向直方图;最后,按权值合并成一个大的梯度方向直方图金字塔作为图像的形状特征。

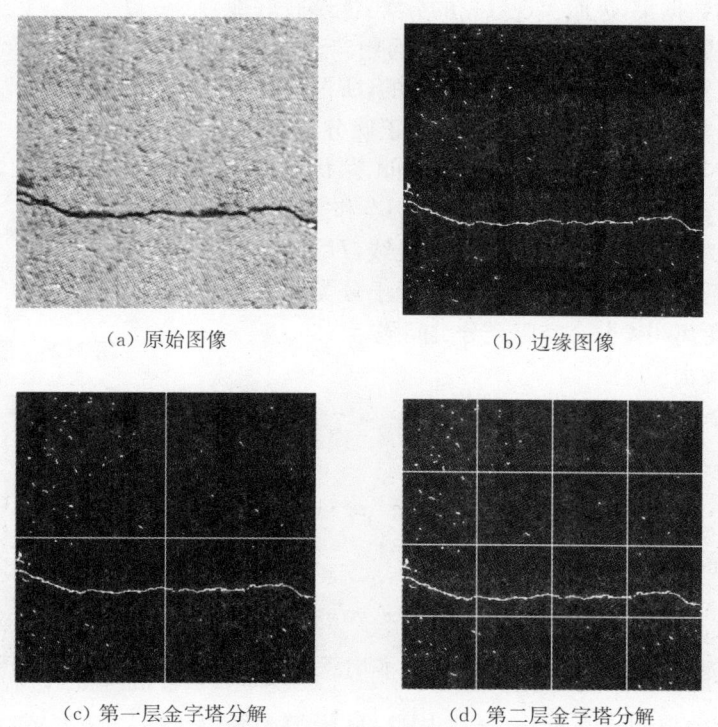

图 3-23 PHOG 特征提取过程

对于图 3-23(a)的路面破损图像进行 3 层 PHOG 特征提取,其 PHOG 描述就是由 3 个梯度方向直方图顺序联结而成的特征向量。第一层 $l=0$ 不进行空间划分,将整个图像作为一个单元计算其梯度方向直方图,其维数为 4;第二层 $l=1$ 时将图像进行四叉树划分,将图像划分为 4 个矩形单元计算其 HOG 特征,其维数为 $4\times 4=16$ 维;第三层 $l=2$ 时将图像分解为 16 个矩形单元计算 HOG,其维数为 $4\times 16=64$,最终形成的直方图是 $l=0,1,2$ 时各 HOG 直方图的顺序组合,则 PHOG 特征维数为 $4+16+64=84$,如图 3-24 所示。

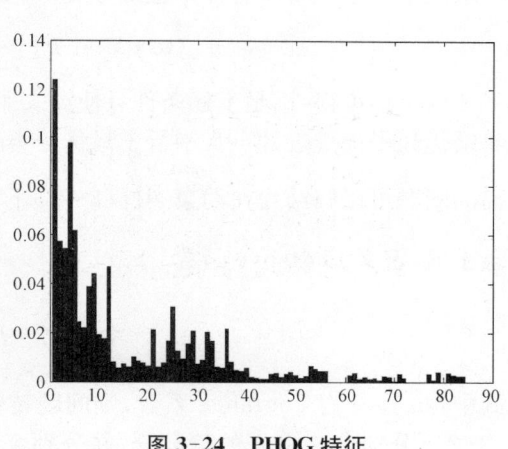

图 3-24 PHOG 特征

3.4 支持向量机分类器

支持向量机(Support Vector Machines,SVMs)分类器是由 Vapnik 等[119]于 1995 年提出的一类新型机器学习方法,该方法通过把低维空间中线性不可分的数据集映射成高维空间中线性可分的数据集,进而实现数据的分类,能够较好地解决小样本、非线性及高维数等模式识别问题。SVMs 是从线性可分情况下的最优分类面发展而来的,所谓最优分类线就是要求分类面不但能够将两类样本正确分开,而且使两类样本的分类间隔最大,推广至高维空间,最优分类线就变成了最优分类面。如图 3-25 所示,实心点和空心点表示两类样本,H 为正确分开两类样本的分类线,H_1,H_2 分别为过各类中离分类线最近的样本且平行于分类线的直线,它们之间的距离叫做分类空隙或分类间隔。

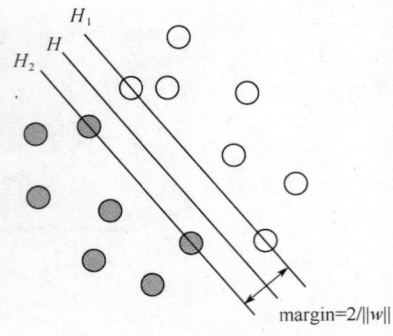

图 3-25 最优分类线

1) 最优分类面

设线性可分的样本集 (x_i, y_i),$i = 1, 2, \cdots, n$,$x \in R^d$,$y \in \{+1, -1\}$ 为类别标号,d 维空间中线性判别函数的一般形式为

$$g(x) = w \cdot x + b \tag{3-21}$$

分类面方程可以描述为

$$w \cdot x + b = 0 \tag{3-22}$$

将判别函数归一化使两类中的所有样本均满足 $|g(x)| \geqslant 1$,即离分类平面最近的样本 $|g(x)| = 1$,则分离间隔等于 $\dfrac{2}{\|w\|}$,因此,间隔最大等价于使 $\|w\|$ 或 $\|w\|^2$ 最小,而要求判别分界面对所有样本正确分类,则要求其满足

$$y_i[(w \cdot x) + b] - 1 \geqslant 0 \quad i = 1, 2, \cdots, n \tag{3-23}$$

由上述可得:满足上述条件且使 $\|w\|^2$ 最小的分类面就是最优分类面。过两类样本中离最优超平面最近的点且平行于最优分类超平面的样本就被称为支持向量,则最优分类平面的问题可以归结为在约束条件(3-23)下,求目标函数 $\varphi(w) = \dfrac{1}{2} \|w\|^2 = \dfrac{1}{2}(w \cdot w)$ 的最小值,定义 Lagrange 函数

$$L(w, b, a) = \frac{1}{2}(w \cdot w) - \sum_{i=1}^{n} a_i \{y_i[(w \cdot x) + b] - 1\} \tag{3-24}$$

其中,$a_i \geqslant 0$ 为 Lagrange 系数,则问题转化为对 w 和 b 求 Lagrange 函数的极小值。对式(3-24)分别求 w 和 b 的偏微分,并分别令其为零,则原问题转化为以下对偶问题,约束条件为

$$\sum_{i=1}^{n} y_i a_i = 0 \tag{3-25}$$

其中,$a_i \geqslant 0$,$i = 1, 2, \cdots, n$,对 a_i 求解式(3-25)函数的最大值:

$$Q(a) = \sum_{i=1}^{n} a_i - \frac{1}{2} \sum_{i,j=1}^{n} a_i a_j y_i y_j (x_i \cdot x_j) \tag{3-26}$$

上式中,如果 a_i^* 为最优解,则有

$$w^* = \sum_{i=1}^{n} a_i^* y_i x_i \quad (3-27)$$

由上式可得:最优分类面的权系数向量是训练样本向量的线性组合,这是一个不等式约束下的二次函数极值问题,存在唯一解。根据 Kuhn-Tucker 条件,该优化问题的解满足

$$a_i(y_i(w \cdot x_i + b) - 1) = 0 \quad i = 1, 2, \cdots, n \quad (3-28)$$

因此,对于多数样本 a_i^* 将为0,取值不为0的 a_i^* 对应于使式(3-4)等号成立的样本,即为支持向量,b^* 可由任意一个支持向量通过式(3-4)等式成立求得,求解上述问题后得到的最优分类函数为

$$f(x) = \text{sgn}\{(w^* \cdot x) + b^*\} = \text{sgn}\Big\{ \sum_{i=1}^{n} a_i^* y_i (x_i \cdot x) + b^* \Big\} \quad (3-29)$$

其中,sgn( ) 为符号函数。由于非支持向量对应的 a_i 均为0,因此式(3-29)中的求和实际上只对支持向量进行。将上述讨论的基于线性可分样本问题推广到非线性可分样本的分类问题,即广义最优化分类平面问题。所谓线性不可分的情况,就是某些训练样本不能满足式(3-23)的条件。为此,添加一个松弛项,则 $\xi_i > 0$ 为

$$y_i[(w \cdot x) + b] - 1 + \xi_i \geqslant 0 \quad (3-30)$$

对于足够小的 $\sigma > 0$,只要使式(3-12)成立,即

$$F_\sigma(\xi_i) = \sum_{i=1}^{n} \xi_i^\sigma \quad (3-31)$$

对应线性可分情况下使分离间隔最大,在线性不可分下可引入约束 $\|w\|^2 \leqslant c_k$,在约束(3-28)和 $\|w\|^2 \leqslant c_k$ 的条件下,求式(3-29)的极小值,就得到了线性不可分情况下的最优分类平面,该平面称为广义最优分类平面。取 $\sigma = 1$,则经过简化计算,广义最优分类平面问题可进一步演化为在条件(3-28)下求下列函数的极小值,即

$$\phi(w, \xi) = \frac{1}{2}(w \cdot w) + C\Big(\sum_{i=1}^{n} \xi_i \Big) \quad (3-32)$$

其中,C 为常数。用于求解最优分类面时同样的方法求解这一最优化问题,同样可以得到一个二次函数极值问题,其结果与可分情况下得到的判别函数相同,只是其 a_i 的约束变为

$$0 \leqslant a_i \leqslant C, i = 1, 2, \cdots, n \quad (3-33)$$

2) 核函数

非线性支持向量机在映射的过程中首先采用一个非线性的变换 ϕ 将输入映射到一个特征空间 Z,即 $X \xrightarrow{\phi R^m \to R^{m_1}} F$。设 $\{\phi_j(X)\}_{j=1}^{m_1}$ 为输入空间 R^m 到输出空间 R^{m_1} 的一组非线性变换,则映射可表示为

$$\phi(X) = [\phi_1(X), \phi_2(X), \cdots, \phi_{m_1}(X)] \quad (3-34)$$

在特征空间 F 中,数据线性可分,则在 F 中可以找到一个线性判别函数对应于 X 中的

一个非线性判别函数。支持向量机可以通过训练来构造一个线性判别函数 $w^T\phi(X)+b=0$，使得分离间隔最大，根据 Hilbert-Schmidt 原理，只要满足 Mercer 条件，可以找到一个核函数 $K(x, x')$，使式(3-35)成立，即

$$K(x, x') = \varphi^T(x)\varphi(x) \tag{3-35}$$

因此，在最优分类面中采用适当的点积函数 $K(x, x')$ 就可以实现某一非线性变换后的线性分类，相应的优化函数为

$$Q(a) = \sum_{i=1}^{n} a_i - \frac{1}{2}\sum_{i,j=1}^{n} a_i a_j y_i y_j K(x_i, x_j) \tag{3-36}$$

而相应的判别函数为

$$f(x) = \text{sgn}\left\{\sum_{i=1}^{n} a_i y_i K(x_i, x) + b\right\} \tag{3-37}$$

对一个特定的核函数，给定的样本集中的任意一个样本都可能成为一个支持向量，因此，采用不同核函数 $K(x_i, x_j)$ 可以构造实现输入空间中不同类型的非线性决策面的学习机。

3.5 实验分析

本文采用本课题组自主研发的 DN-2011 型车载便携式公路路面病害检测设备采集路面图像，利用同态滤波[115]对采集的路面图像进行光照均衡处理，以构建东南大学路面图像数据库。同态滤波是把频率过滤和灰度变换结合起来的一种图像处理方法，该方法首先对图像进行对数变换，实现对图像的灰度拉伸，然后对经过对数处理后的图像进行傅里叶变换，将图像转换到频率域，并通过对图像进行频域滤波实现图像的去噪处理，最后，对图像进行傅里叶逆变换和指数运算即得到同态滤波处理后的图像。构建的东南大学路面图像数据库如图 3-26 所示，图像共 140 幅，图像大小为 512×512，包括横裂、纵裂、网裂和正常路面四种类型，每种类型 35 张，保证了数据库中样本的均衡性。

(a) 横裂

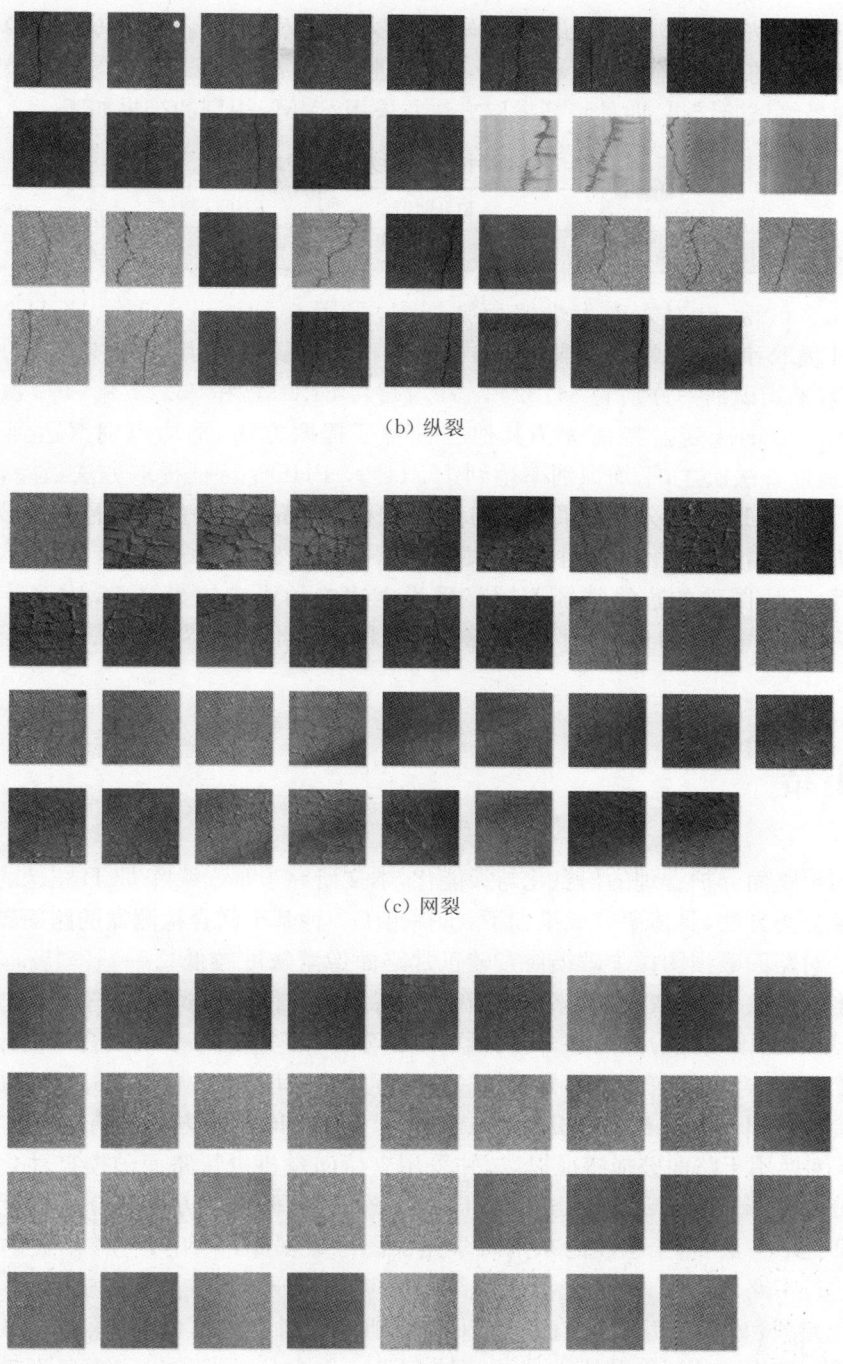

(b) 纵裂

(c) 网裂

(d) 正常

图 3-26 东南大学路面图像数据库

随机选取东南大学路面数据库中 80% 图像(112 张)做训练样本,其余剩余的 20% 图像(28 张)做测试样本,分别采用 Contourlet 变换、EOH 特征提取、PHOG 特征提取和 HOG

特征提取四种方法提取样本图像的特征向量,并采用 SVMs 进行分类识别,SVMs 核函数选取实时性较好的线性核函数 $k(x,y)=x \cdot y$。进行 100 次随机试验,并求 100 次随机试验的结果作为最终试验结果,四种特征提取方法并采用 SVMs 识别的结果如表 3.2 所示。

表 3.2 四种特征提取方法识别结果

特征种类	Contourlet 特征	EOH 特征	PHOG 特征	HOG 特征
识别率	84.32%	75.14%	51.93%	73.25%

由表 3.2 可得:针对东南大学路面数据库,采用 Contourlet 变换、EOH 特征提取、PHOG 特征提取和 HOG 特征提取四种方法进行特征提取,并选用线性核函数的 SVMs 进行识别实验,平均识别率分别为 84.32%、75.14%、51.93% 和 73.25%。100 次随机试验结果表明 Contourlet 变换特征优于其他三种特征提取方法,平均识别率达到 84.32%,EOH 特征提取方法次之,平均识别率达到 75.14%,PHOG 特征提取方法最差,平均识别率仅为 51.93%。PHOG 分类结果较低的主要原因是路面图像中的破损目标区域相对于非破损区域所占整幅图像的比例较小,则获取的边缘图像中破损目标所占区域较小,细分为各子块图像后,子块图像的边缘特征不明显受噪声边缘的影响较为严重,从而导致最终的 PHOG 组合边缘梯度方向直方图特征对路面破损的描述不够详尽,造成最终的识别分类结果较低。

3.6 小结

为了实现路面养护管理的信息化与智能化,本文研究了基于线阵 CCD 图像的路面破损自动检测及分类方法,具体研究成果如下:①提出了一种基于联合检测器的路面破损自动检测方法。针对路面破损图像中破损像素较正常路面像素灰度较低这一基本特征,对比分析了领域灰度差分法、局部灰度最小分析法和分块标记法的优势和弱点,基于级联分类器的思想,提出了用于路面破损检测的联合检测器,理论分析和实验结果表明联合检测器的性能优于领域灰度差分法、局部灰度最小分析法和分块标记法,其检测率达到 96.7%,并研究基于连通域融合的路面破损目标精确定位方法,通过实验验证了该方法的有效性。②提出将 Contourlet 变换用于路面破损特征提取,并采用支持向量机进行路面破损自动化分类的方法。对比分析了 Contourlet 变换、边缘方向直方图、方向梯度直方图和分层梯度方向直方图四种特征提取方法,基于构建的东南大学路面图像数据库,采用线性核函数的 SVMs 作为分类器进行了路面破损识别实验,实验结果表明 Contourlet 变换优于边缘方向直方图、方向梯度直方图和分层梯度方向直方图,平均识别率达到 84.32%。因此,采用 Contourlet 变换进行路面破损特征提取及线性核函数的 SVMs 作为分类器可以实现路面破损类型的有效识别。③提出了一种基于联合特征及随机子空间交叉内核支持向量机分类器集成的路面破损自动化分类方法。研究了图像联合特征的融合策略,基于串行融合策略构造了路面破损图像的 Contourlet 变换和 EOH 联合特征,并基于分类器集成的构造原则实现了交叉内核支持向量机类器的集成方案,采用东南大学路面图像数据库进行了实验,实验结果表明

Contourlet 变换和 EOH 联合特征及随机子空间交叉内核支持向量机分类器集成优于单一 Contoulet 变换特征和 EOH 特征,分类正确率达到 86.61%。

  本文研究了基于线阵 CCD 图像的路面破损自动检测及分类方法,取得了上述研究成果,但是仍然有许多需要进一步深入研究的工作,简要的讨论如下:①路面图像的预处理工作。由于获取的路面图像受噪声及不均匀光照的影响,需要对图像进行预处理工作,本文从工程应用的角度出发对路面图像的预处理进行了简单的预处理研究,从理论研究的角度出发,图像的预处理工作仍需要进一步的深入研究,以尽可能地增强图像目标,为后期的目标检测提供基础。②路面图像的特征提取和识别分类。特征提取及分类始终是图像处理领域研究的热点问题,本文采用了 Contourlet 轮廓特征和几种梯度直方图特征进行路面图像特征描述。如何提高特征描述的精确性及分类算法的效率一直是图像处理需要深入研究的问题,在后续的研究中可以从其他特征描述角度对图像进行特征描述,提高最终的识别分类率。③图像的识别分类。对于图像的识别分类,本文提出了集成分类器的构想,构建的集成分类器是同类型分类器的集成,后续的算法研究过程中,可以尝试采用多类型不同分类器的集成方法,以提高对路面破损图像的分类结果。

下 篇
驾驶人疲劳及异常行为信息感知

Chapter 4

Introduction of Driver's Fatigue and Abnormal Activities Detection

4.1　Introduction of driver's fatigue detection

The phenomenon of fatigue refers to a combination of symptoms such as impaired performance and a subjective feeling of drowsiness. Studies show that 25%~30% of driving accidents are fatigue related[120, 121]. The European Transport Safety Council (ETSC) defines four levels of sleepiness based on behavioral terms as follows: completely awake, moderate sleepiness, severe sleepiness, and sleep[122]. In an attempt to avoid having an accident, most sleepy drivers will try to fight against sleep with moderate sleepiness, severe sleepiness. The purpose of the Driver Fatigue Monitoring System (DFMS) is to monitor the attention status of the driver. If driver fatigue is detected, different countermeasures should be taken to maintain driving safety, depending on the types and levels of fatigue. When a driver is fatigued, certain physical and physiological phenomena can be observed, including changes in brain waves or EEG, eye activity, facial expressions, head nodding, body sagging posture, heart rate, pulse, skin electric potential, gripping force on the steering wheel, and other changes in body activities.

Biological measures of driver's fatigue include Electroencephalogram(EEG), Electrocardiogram (ECG), Electro-oculography (EOG), and surface Electromyogram (sEMG). These signals are collected through electrodes in contact with the skin of the human body. Recent research has proposed various methods of extracting features from a segment of raw EEG data for fatigue detection. Lin et al established a linear regression model to estimate the drowsiness level from the Independent Component Analysis (ICA) of 33-channel EEG signals and could estimate the drowsiness level with 87% accuracy[123]. They then implemented a real-time embedded EEG-based driver drowsiness estimate system[124], which adopted only four channels of EEG data. Damousis et al selected eight eye activity features, extracted from EOG, to develop a Fuzzy Expert System (FES) for the detection of hypovigilance[125]. Jap et al accessed four electroencephalography (EEG) activities for 52 subjects during a monotonous driving session, and the results showed an increase in the ratio of slow wave to fast wave EEG activities over time[126]. Yeo et al trained SVM to classify EEG signals into four principal frequency bands and then to predict the transition from alertness to drowsiness[127]. Hu and Zheng employed a SVM to perform drowsiness prediction with 11 eyelid-related features extracted from EOG[128]. In reference[129], Kernel Principal Component Analysis (KPCA) algorithm was employed to extract nonlinear features from the complexity parameters of EEG and improve the generalization performance of a HMM. Yang et al employed a dynamic BN with EEG and ECG to estimate fatigue, and a first-order HMM was employed to compute the dynamics of a BN at two different time slices[130]. Sibsambhu et al presents a method based on a class of entropy measures on the recorded EEG signals of human subjects for relative quantification of fatigue during driving[131]. Rami et al developed an efficient fuzzy mutual-information-based wavelet packet transform feature-extraction method for classifying the driver drowsiness state into one of predefined drowsiness levels[132].

Physical measures of driver's fatigue include Eye Closure Duration (ECD), blink frequency, nodding frequency, fixed gaze, and frontal face pose. In[133], the different linguistic terms and their corresponding fuzzy sets were distributed in each of the inputs using induced knowledge based on the hierarchical fuzzy partitioning method, and three variables (fixed gaze, PERCLOS, and ECD) were determined to be crucial cues for detecting a driver's fatigue. Suzuki et al derived the following three factors from the blinking waveform[134], and these factors were then weighted using a multiple regression analysis for each individual to calculate the drowsiness level. Orazio et al used a mixture Gaussian model to model the "normal behavior" statistics from the ECD and frequency of eye closure (FEC) for each person to identify anomalous behaviors[135]. Friedrichs and Yang explored 18 features of eye movement for drowsiness detection[136], and chose the Sequential Floating Forward Selection (SFFS) algorithm to select the most promising features to construct a classifier. In reference[137], it also reported that sleep deprived drivers have a lower frequency of steering reversals, a deterioration of steering performance, a decrease in the steering-wheel reversing rate, more frequent steering maneuvers during wakeful periods, no steering correction for a prolonged period of time followed by a jerky motion during drowsy periods, low-velocity steering, large amplitude steering-wheel movements, and large standard deviations in the steering-wheel angle.

Most of the above measures techniques require that sensor devices must be attached to driver's clothing or body, which is not a natural way to monitor a driver's activities. It is unlikely that drivers would accept any tethered sensing solution, i.e. using wired sensors or wireless sensors attached to their bodies. Image-based fatigue detection would be more applicable in a consumer car without the requirement of special markers or user intervention. Eskandarian et al utilized Artificial Neural Network (ANN) to analyze vehicle parameter data and eye-closure data to infer driver fatigue, and then, they analyzed the data to identify the potential variables that were correlated with drowsiness[138]. Fan et al utilized a gabor features representation of the face for fatigue detection[139], and then AdaBoost algorithm was used to extract the most critical features from the dynamic feature set and construct a strong classifier for fatigue detection. But a few of recent works attempt to recognize and classify fatigue degrees of vehicle's drivers using image-based technologies.

4.2 Introduction of driver's abnormal activities detection

The driver's behaviours reflect his or her driving conditions, such as fatigue levels, attention and other unsafe information. Automatic understanding and characterizing driver behaviours is one of the key aspects for the development of human-centered driver assistance systems, in which Intelligent Transportation System Community (ITSC) has been very interested. The driver's unsafe behaviours such as eating, talking on a cellular telephone and fatigue, will reduce a driver's alertness to the vehicle's surrounding environment. Nadeau et al[140] carried out an epidemiological study on two large cohorts, namely non-users and users of cellphones, and the most significant finding is that the adjusted relative risks for heavy users were at least two times to those making minimal use of cellphones. To develop an effective driver behaviour recognition system, two important techniques have to be included, i.e., how to efficiently describe a driver's postures or maneuvers, and how to reliably classify the postures accordingly.

The driver's body information can be obtained in untethered manner by using vision sensors. Liu et al[141] described a vision system that tracked the driver's face and estimated his face pose in driving conditions by using the yaw orientation angles. In order to address the problem of lacking the stable illumination in driving images captured by the colour camera, Kato et al[142] developed an active capturing system with a far infrared camera for the detection of the driver face directions, such as rightward, frontward and leftward. Cheng et al[143] used a commercial motion-capture system with the retroreflective markers placed on the driver's head, left hand and right hand, to predict and recognize the driver's left and right intersection-turn behaviours. Watta et al[144] presented a vision system to recognize the driver's seven poses including looking over the left shoulder or over the right shoulder, at the road ahead, down at the instrument panel, at the center rear view mirror, at the left rear view mirror or at the right rear view mirror. Cheng et al[145] introduced a multiple camera views (i.e., thermal infrared and colour) and multi-modal video-based system to recognize the driver's activities, including going forward, turning left or turning right. Demirdjian et al[146] used an infrared Time-of-Flight (TOF) camera to estimate the orientation and location of a driver's limbs, including hands, arms, head and torso, and the articulated ICP algorithm and 3D model fitting approach were applied to incorporate the uncertainty in visual observation and model data in the driving pose estimation framework. Also, Yang et al[147] presented an ECG system to monitor the driver's sitting postures (forward movement, back movement, left back movement or right back).

Most of the current research literatures for driver's activity recognition focused on the detection of driver's head orientation, face direction and gaze, etc. Although many other kinds of motion-capture technologies exist in the literature to recover body pose by using different kind of sensors, like magnetic, mechanical or optical marker-based sensors to provide either three degrees-of-freedom position of a point on the subject's body or full six DOF body-part orientation and position, such techniques have the biggest disadvantage that a subject is required to attach the sensor device or markers with his/her body or cloth, which is not a natural way of monitoring a driver's activities. So, it is unlikely that drivers would accept any tethered sensing solution, i.e. using wireless sensors or wired sensors attached to the driver's body. For this reason, image-based motion capture would be more applicable in a consumer car, as it does not require special markers or user intervention. A few of recent works attempted to understand and recognize the driver's postures, such as grasping the steel wheel, operating the shift lever, eating a cake and talking on a cellular telephone by using the image-based system. Only Veeraraghavan et al[148] proposed an agglomerative clustering and a Bayesian Eigen-image classifier to recognize two types of a driver postures: unsafe type and safe type with a side-mounted camera capturing the driver's profile.

Chapter 5
Perception of Driver's Fatigue Information

A decisive step in developing image-based driver fatigue degree recognition system is to extract suitable features from the driver's images and characterize differences between different driver's fatigue expressions. In this paper, we proposed an efficient features extraction of driver's fatigue expression based curvelet transform, and Support Vector Machines (SVM) was then exploited in classification fatigue expression, compared with Linear Perception (LP) Classifier, k-Nearest Neighbor (kNN) classifier, Multilayer Perception (MLP) classifier and Parzen classifier.

5.1 SEU fatigue expression data acquisition

Traffic accidents are often related with moderate sleepiness and severe sleepiness. The symptoms of moderate sleepiness is that vehicle drivers repeat yawning, and the symptoms of severe sleepiness is that vehicle drivers have difficulties in keeping eyes open and nodding off at the wheel. So our SEU fatigue expression dataset, created in southeast university using a side-mounted Logitech C905 CCD camera, consists of three kinds of facial expressions, i. e., awake expressions, moderate fatigue expressions, and severe fatigue expressions. There are 20 male drivers and 20 female drivers in SEU fatigue expression dataset, and the lighting conditions varied under the natural conditions, as the car was in an outdoor parking lot. The Fig. 5.1 shows example images of a driver inside the vehicle.

        (a)   (b)   (c)

Fig. 5.1 Example images of a driver inside the vehicle

In this paper, Viola-Jones face detection algorithm was used to detect the vehicle driver's faces[149]. The basic principle of the Viola-Jones algorithm is to scan a sub-window capable of detecting faces across a given input image, and the standard image processing approach would be to rescale the input image to different sizes and then run the fixed size detector through these images. The major contributions of Viola-Jones face detection algorithm consist of rectangular feature extraction, classification using AdaBoost learning algorithm, and multi-scale detection algorithm. The face detection result of one example images of a driver inside the vehicle is shown in Fig. 5.2.

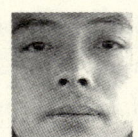

(a) Example image   (b) Result image

Fig. 5.2 Face detection and segmentation of a vehicle driver

5.2 Curvelet transform for image feature description

In order to address the problem of illumination variations in images of SEU fatigue facial expression dataset, we adopted the well-known normalization technique called Homomorphic Filter (HOMOF) to enhance the image quality. With HOMOF, the images are first transformed into logarithm and then a frequency domain to emphasize the high frequency components. Then the images are transformed back into spatial domain by applying the inverse Fourier transform, followed by appropriate exponential operation. One example image of SEU fatigue facial expression dataset, before and after preprocessed by HOMOF is shown in Fig. 5.3.

(a) Before preprocessed   (b) After preprocessed

Fig. 5.3 Example image before and after preprocessed by HOMOF

Curvelet transform[150, 151] is one of the latest developments of non-adaptive transforms. Compared to wavelet, curvelet provides a more sparse representation of the image, with improved directional elements and better ability to represent edges and other singularities along curves. Compared to methods based on orthonormal transforms or direct time domain processing, sparse representation usually offers better performance with its capacity for efficient signal modelling.

While wavelets generalize the Fourier transform by using a basis that represents both location and spatial frequency, the curvelet transform provides the flexibility that the degree of localization in orientation varies with scale. In curvelet, fine scale basis functions are long ridges, and the shape of the basis functions at scale j is 2^{-j} by $2^{-j/2}$. So the finescale bases are skinny ridges with a precisely determined orientation. The curvelet coefficients can be expressed by

$$c(j, l, k) = \int_{R^2} f(x)\phi_{j,l,k}(x)\mathrm{d}x \qquad (5-1)$$

where $\phi_{j,l,k}(\cdot)$ denotes curvelet function, and j, l and k are the variable of scale, orientation, and position respectively. In the last few years, several discrete curvelet and curvelet-like transforms have been proposed. The influential approach is based on the Fast Fourier Transform (FFT)[152]. In the frequency domain, the curvelet transform can be implemented with ϕ by means of the window function U. Defining a pair of windows $W(r)$ (a radial window) and $V(t)$ (an angular window) as below

$$\sum_{j=-\infty}^{\infty} W^2(2^j r) = 1, \quad r \in (3/4, \ 3/2) \qquad (5-2)$$

$$\sum_{j=-\infty}^{\infty} V^2(t-1) = 1, \quad r \in (-1/2, \ 1/2) \qquad (5-3)$$

where variables W as a frequency domain variable, and r and θ as polar coordinates in the frequency domain, then for each $j \geqslant j_0$, U_j is defined in the Fourier domain by

$$U_j(r, \theta) = 2^{3j/4}\omega(2^{-j}r)v\left(\frac{2^{[j/2]}\theta}{2\pi}\right) \qquad (5-4)$$

where $[j/2]$ denotes the integer part of $j/2$. The above brief introduction of the frequency plane partitioning into radial and angular divisions can be explained by Fig. 5.4, where the shaded area is one of the polar wedges represented by U_j, which is supported by the radial and angular windows W and V. The radial divisions (concentric circles) are responsible for decomposition of the image in multiple scales (used for bandpassing the image) and angular divisions corresponding to different angles or orientation. Therefore when we consider each wedge like the shaded one, one needs to define the scale and angle to analyze the bandpassed image at scale j and angle θ. The technical details of the curvelet transform implementation is much involved and beyond the scope of current paper. The fastest curvelet transform currently available is vurvelets via wrapping[153], which will be used for our work. If $f([t_1, t_2])$, $0 \leqslant t_1, t_2 \leqslant n$ is taken to be a Cartesian array and $\hat{f}[n_1, n_2]$ to denote its 2D Discrete Fourier Transform.

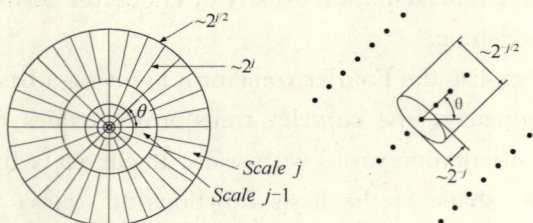

Fig. 5.4 Curvelet transform: Fourier frequency domain partitioning (left) and spatial domain representation of a wedge (right)

From the curvelet coefficients, some statistics can be calculated from each of these curvelet sub-bands as image descriptor. The mean μ and standard deviation δ are the convenient features[154]. If n curvelets are used for the transform, $2n$ features $G = [G_\mu, G_\delta]$ are obtained, where $G_\mu = [\mu_1, \mu_2, \cdots, \mu_n]$, $G_\delta = [\delta_1, \delta_2, \cdots, \delta_n]$. The $2n$ dimension feature vector can be used to represent each image in the dataset. Curvelet transform of one example image of Fig. 3 is shown in Fig. 5.5, and Fig. 5.5(b) is the approximate coefficients, and Fig. 5.5(c)~Fig. 5.5(j) are detailed coefficients at eight angles from three scales. All the images are rescaled to same dimension for demonstration purpose. From each of the detail coefficient matrices, the first-order and second-order statistics mean and standard deviation were calculated as features vectors of fatigue expressions of vehicle drivers in this paper.

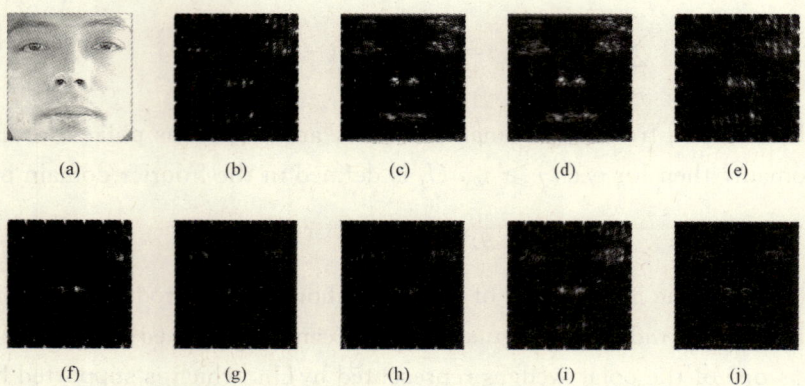

Fig. 5.5 Curvelet transform of example image

5.3 Support Vector Machines (SVMs)

SVMs were originally designed for binary-class classification problems[46], based on the idea of structural risk minimization. The basic principle of binary-class SVMs is to find an Optimal Separating Hyperplane (OSH) and separate two classes of patterns based on the training set and the decision boundary, which can be formulated as a Quadratic Programming (QP) problem in the feature space[155]. Consider a problem of separating training data $\{(x_i, y_i)\}_{i=1}^{N}$ into two separate classes, where $x_i \subset \Re^n$ is an ith input vector in n-dimensional input space, and $y_i \in \{+1, -1\}$ is a specified binary target vector. The main goal of SVMs approach is to find a hyperplane as following

$$f(x_i) = \langle w \cdot x_i \rangle + b \tag{5-5}$$

where w is the weight vector and b is a bias term. The hyperplane is able to separate the class linearly so that all the points with the same class are on the same side of the hyperplane. According to the hyperplane, all the training data must satisfy the following constrains

$$\begin{cases} \langle w \cdot x_i \rangle + b \geqslant +1 & \text{for} \quad y_i = +1 \\ \langle w \cdot x_i \rangle + b \leqslant -1 & \text{for} \quad y_i = -1 \end{cases} \tag{5-6}$$

Each sample is classified into $+1$ or -1 which side of the hyperplane lies on. The constraint of the hyperplane can be written as:

$$y_i(w \cdot x_i) + b \geqslant 1, \quad i = 1, 2, \cdots, N \tag{5-7}$$

The distance from the closest point to the hyperplane equals to $1/\|w\|$, where $\|\cdot\|$ is the Euclidean Norm function, and the hyperplane realizes the maximal hyperplane with the margin $\rho = 2/\|w\|$. The margin ρ can be seen as a measure of the generalization ability of the hyperplane classification. The OSH is the separating hyperplane to maximize the margin ρ. Accordingly, it corresponds to minimizing the Euclidean norm of the weight vector. On the other hand, for the non-separable case, the slack variables ξ_i allowing the margin to be violated can be introduced

$$y_i(\langle w^T \cdot x_i \rangle + b) \geqslant 1 - \xi_i \tag{5-8}$$

where the slack variable ξ_i, $i = 1, \cdots, N$, is a measure of the misclassification errors, namely when the ith input vector is misclassified by the hyperplane, the corresponding $\xi_i > 0$. From the structural risk minimization inductive principle, the binary-class SVMs approach is to minimize the guaranteed risk bound as follows:

$$\min_{w, b, \xi} \frac{1}{2} \langle w^T \cdot w \rangle + C \sum_{i=1}^{N} \xi_i \tag{5-9}$$

where C is a user-defined positive finite constant, controlling a compromise between maximizing the margin and minimizing the number of training set error. A larger C means that a higher penalty is assigned to empirical errors. The solution to the optimization problem of equation (5-9) is a convex QP, which can be solved by using the langrage multipliers method and the Karush-Kuhn-Tucher theorem in the optimization theory. Accordingly, the coefficient α_i can be found by solving the flowing convex QP problem

$$\alpha^* = \arg \max_\alpha \left[\sum_{i=1}^N \alpha_i - \frac{1}{2} \sum_{i=1}^N \sum_{j=1}^N \alpha_i \alpha_j y_i y_j (\boldsymbol{x}_i \cdot \boldsymbol{x}_j) \right] \quad (5-10)$$

with constraints as following

$$\sum_{i=1}^N \alpha_i y_i = 0, \quad C \geqslant \alpha_i \geqslant 0, \quad i = 1, 2, \cdots, N \quad (5-11)$$

Therefore the decision boundary function of the classifier can be expressed as

$$f(\boldsymbol{x}) = \mathrm{sign}\left[\sum_{i=1}^N \alpha_i y_i \langle \boldsymbol{x}_i \cdot \boldsymbol{x} \rangle + b \right] \quad (5-12)$$

The formulated binary-class SVMs is called the hard margin SVMs. However, the hardmargin SVMs do not work well, while the training data are linearly inseparable. One improvement is the nonlinear SVMs that maps the training data from the input space into a high-dimensional feature space via a non-linear mapping function $\Phi(\cdot)$, also called the kernel function such that

$$K(\boldsymbol{x}_i, \boldsymbol{x}_j) = \langle \boldsymbol{x}_i, \boldsymbol{x}_j \rangle = \langle \Phi(\boldsymbol{x}_i) \cdot \Phi(\boldsymbol{x}_j) \rangle \quad (5-13)$$

The interesting property of nonlinear SVMs is that, once a valid kernel function has been selected, one can practically work in spaces of any dimension without any significant additional computational cost, since feature mapping is never effectively performed. The most commonly applied nonlinear kernel is linear kernel, polynomial kernel, RBF kernel, sigmoid kernel, and intersection kernel, these nonlinear kernels are described as follows.

Linear kernel

$$K(\boldsymbol{x}_i, \boldsymbol{x}_j) = \boldsymbol{x}_i^T \cdot \boldsymbol{x}_j \quad (5-14)$$

Polynomial kernel

$$K(\boldsymbol{x}_i, \boldsymbol{x}_j) = (\gamma \cdot \boldsymbol{x}_i^T \cdot \boldsymbol{x}_j + r)^d, \quad \gamma > 0 \quad (5-15)$$

RBF kernel

$$K(\boldsymbol{x}_i, \boldsymbol{x}_j) = \exp(-\gamma \parallel \boldsymbol{x}_i - \boldsymbol{x}_j \parallel^2), \quad \gamma > 0 \quad (5-16)$$

Sigmoid kernel

$$K(\boldsymbol{x}_i, \boldsymbol{x}_j) = \tanh(\gamma \cdot \boldsymbol{x}_i^T \boldsymbol{x}_j + r), \quad \gamma > 0 \quad (5-17)$$

Intersection kernel

$$K(\boldsymbol{x}_i, \boldsymbol{x}_j) = \min(\boldsymbol{x}_i, \boldsymbol{x}_j) \tag{5-18}$$

where γ, r and d are kernel parameters. The decision boundary function can be rewritten as

$$f(\boldsymbol{x}) = \text{sign}\left[\sum_{i=1}^{N} \alpha_i y_i K(\boldsymbol{x}_i, \boldsymbol{x}) + b\right] \tag{5-19}$$

Therefore, the dual objective function in a non-linear SVMs becomes as follows:

$$\alpha^* = \arg\max_{\alpha}\left[\sum_{i=1}^{N} \alpha_i - \frac{1}{2}\sum_{i=1}^{N}\sum_{j=1}^{N} \alpha_i \alpha_j y_i y_j K(\boldsymbol{x}_i \cdot \boldsymbol{x}_j)\right] \tag{5-20}$$

The Karush-Kuhn-Tucker (KKT) conditions are necessary and sufficient conditions for an optimal point of a positive definite dual problem. The dual problem is as follows

$$\begin{cases} \alpha_i = 0 \Rightarrow y_i f(\boldsymbol{x}_i) \geqslant 1 \\ 0 < \alpha_i < C \Rightarrow y_i f(\boldsymbol{x}_i) = 1 \\ \alpha_i = C \Rightarrow y_i f(\boldsymbol{x}_i) \leqslant 1 \end{cases} \tag{5-21}$$

The dual objective function is usually solved by the sequential minimization optimization (SMO) algorithm[156]. Even though binary-class SVMs shows the excellent performance in pattern classification applications, it is required to formulate a multi-class SVMs method since most of classifying applications are considered as the multi-category problems in the real world. Multi-class pattern recognition problems are commonly solved by using a combination of binary-class SVMs and a decision strategy to decide the multi-class of the input pattern. This implementation of k-class OAO SVMs is converted into k binary SVMs problems[157, 158], and then combine k binary classifiers. The ith SVMs is trained with all samples in the ith class with positive label, and all other samples with negative label. Considering the training set $\{(x_i, y_i)\}_{i=1}^{N}$, where $x_i \in R^n$ is given a class label $y_i \in \{1, \cdots, k\}$. The k-class OAA SVMs of the ith class can be expressed into the following problem:

$$\min_{w^i, b^i, \xi_j^i} \left\{\frac{1}{2}\|w^i\|^2 + C\sum_{j=1}^{N} \xi_j^i\right\} \tag{5-22}$$

subject to

$$\begin{matrix} (w^i)^T \varphi(\boldsymbol{x}_j) + b^i \geqslant 1 - \xi_j^i & \text{if} & y_j = i \\ (w^i)^T \varphi(\boldsymbol{x}_j) + b^i \leqslant -1 + \xi_j^i & \text{if} & y_j \neq i \end{matrix} \quad \xi_j^i \geqslant 0, j = 1, \cdots, N \tag{5-23}$$

We can assign the data x_j belongs to the class c_i with the maximal value of the decision function based on the following equation.

$$c_i = \arg\max_{i=1,\cdots,k} ((w^i)^T \varphi_i(\boldsymbol{x}_j) + b^i) \tag{5-24}$$

5.4 Other classification methods compared

1) Linear perception (LP) classifier

The linear perceptron (LP) classifier can be seen as a simplest kind of feedforward neural network[159], which is shown in Fig. 5.6. A feature representation function $f(x_i, Y_j)$ maps each possible input/output pair to a finite-dimensional real-valued feature vector.

$$\hat{Y}_j = \arg\max_{Y_j} \{f(\boldsymbol{x}_i, Y_j) \cdot \boldsymbol{w}\} \quad (5-25)$$

where $\boldsymbol{w}$ is a weight vector. Learning again iterates over the samples, predicting an output for each, leaving the weights unchanged when the predicted output matches the target, and changing them when it does not. The update becomes

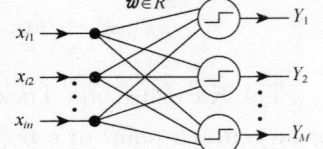

Fig. 5.6 Linear perceptron classifier network

$$\boldsymbol{w}_{t+1} = \boldsymbol{w}_t + f(\boldsymbol{x}_i, Y_j) - f(\boldsymbol{x}_i, \hat{Y}_j) \quad (5-26)$$

This multi-class formulation reduces to the original perception when $\boldsymbol{x}_i$ is a real-valued vector, Y_j is chosen from $\{0, 1\}$, and $f(\boldsymbol{x}_i, Y_j) = Y_j \cdot \boldsymbol{x}_i$. For certain problems, input/output representations and features can be chosen so that $\arg\max_{Y_j} \{f(\boldsymbol{x}_i, Y_j) \cdot \boldsymbol{w}\}$ can be found efficiently even though Y_j is chosen from a very large or even infinite set.

2) k-Nearest Neighbor (kNN) classifier

k-Nearest Neighbor (kNN) classifer[160] is a method for classifying objects based on closest training examples in the feature space. kNN is a type of instance-based learning, or lazy learning where the function is only approximated locally and all computation is defered until classification. The k-nearest neighbor algorithm is amongst the simplest of all machine learning algorithms: an object is classified by a majority vote of its neighbors, with the object being assigned to the class most common amongst its k nearest neighbors (k is a positive integer, typically small). If k=1, then the object is simply assigned to the class of its nearest neighbor. The kNN rule is optimal in the asymptotic case, i.e., the error tends to the Bayes error when the size of the training set tends to infinity. The major drawback of the kNN algorithm is the computational complexity, caused by the large number of distance computations.

3) Multilayer perception (MLP) classifier

Multilayer perception (MLP) classifier is a modification of the standard linear perceptron, which can distinguish data that is not linearly separable. A multilayer perceptron is a feedforward artificial neural network model that maps sets of input data onto a set of appropriate output, and consists of a set of source nodes forming the input layer, one or more hidden layers of computation nodes, and an output layer of nodes[161].

The MLP utilizes a supervised learning technique called backpropagation for training the network and constructs input-output mappings that are a nested composition of nonlinearities with the form

$$y = f(\sum g(\sum (\cdot))) \quad (5-27)$$

where the number of function compositions is given by the number of network layers. An MLP can be trained by gradient descent using the back-propagation algorithm to optimize any derivable criterion, such as the Mean Squared Error. Here, an MLP is trained to classify an input to be one of the given class labels. The input of the MLP is a vector corresponding to the features extracted from gait patterns. The output of the MLP is either 1 (if the input corresponds to a control group) or −1 (if the input corresponds to children with CP). Though MLPs have been proved to be able to virtually approximate any function with any desired accuracy, there is a common criticism for MLP that is very difficult to interpret the trained discriminant function.

4) Parzen classifier

Parzen classifier is a kernel density estimator, with which a nonlinear function is approximated by the superposition of a set of kernels[162]. For pattern x_j, a Gaussian kernel-based Parzen classifier is determined by N training samples $X = [X_1, X_2, \cdots, X_N]$ as follows:

$$f(x_j, s) = \frac{1}{N} \sum_{i=1}^{N} \frac{1}{(s\sqrt{2\pi})^n} \exp\left(-\frac{\|x_j - x_i\|^2}{2s^2}\right) \quad (5-28)$$

where x_i is an n-dimensions training feature vector of training sample X_i, and s is a kernel width. The Parzen classifier design means to estimate the relevant kernel width s using the training feature set $\{x_1, \cdots, x_i, \cdots, x_N\}$. A maximum likelihood principle was adopted to estimate the kernel width s which is as follows:

$$s = \sqrt{\frac{1}{n \cdot N} \sum_{j=1}^{N} \sum_{i \neq j}^{N} \frac{\|x_j - x_i\|^2}{N-1}} \quad (5-29)$$

5.5 Experiments

Two standard experimental procedures, named the holdout approach and the cross-validation approach, are used to compare the performance of SVMs with five different kernels and other four classifiers, namely, LP classifier, kNN classifier, MLP classifier, and Parzen classifier by using HP Elite Book 6930p computer. In the holdout approach, certain amounts of fatigue facial expression features extracted from images in SEU fatigue facial expression dataset (shown in Fig. 5.7) are reserved for testing, and the rest are for training. In k-fold cross-validation approach, SEU fatigue facial expression dataset is partitioned into k sub-datasets. Of them, the kth sub-dataset is retained for testing the classification model and the remaining $k-1$ sub-datasets are used for training the classification model. The cross-validation experiments are then repeated k times, with all of the k sub-samples used exactly once as the validation dataset[163]. The k experiment results from the folds are then averaged to produce a single classification rate.

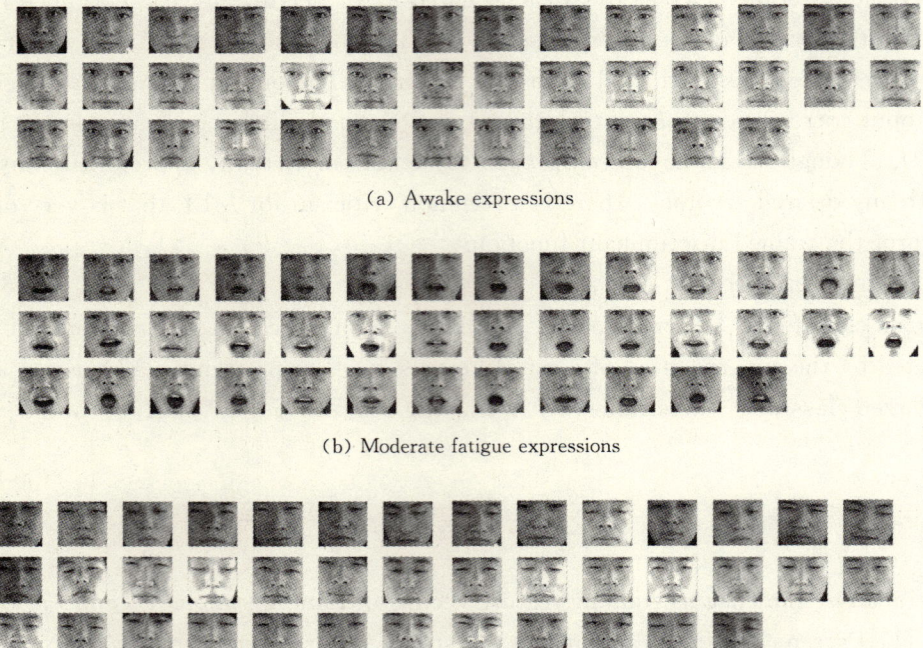

(a) Awake expressions

(b) Moderate fatigue expressions

(c) Severe fatigue expressions

Fig. 5.7 Fatigue facial expression of vehicle drivers in SEU fatigue facial expression dataset

1) Holdup experiments

Holdout experiments are based on randomly dividing fatigue expressions features into a training dataset (80% of fatigue expression features extracted from the images in SEU fatigue expression dataset) and a test dataset (20% of fatigue expression features extracted from the images in SEU fatigue expression dataset). Using the holdout experiment approach, only the test dataset is used to estimate the generalization error. We repeated the holdout experiment 100 times by randomly splitting the fatigue expression dataset, and recorded the classification results.

In the first holdout experiment, the same set of training and testing are applied to SVMs with five different kernels, and their classification performances are simultaneously compared. The results of classification rate for fatigue expressions by SVMs with five different kernels are displayed in the bar plots of Fig. 5.8(a) and box plots of Fig. 5.8(b). The average classification accuracies of linear kernel, polynomial kernel, RBF kernel, sigmoid kernel and intersection kernel are 82.96%, 85.21%, 33.79%, 25.04% and 84.08%, respectively. From Fig. 5.8, it is obvious that SVMs with polynomial kernel offers the best performance among the five kernels in the first holdout experiments.

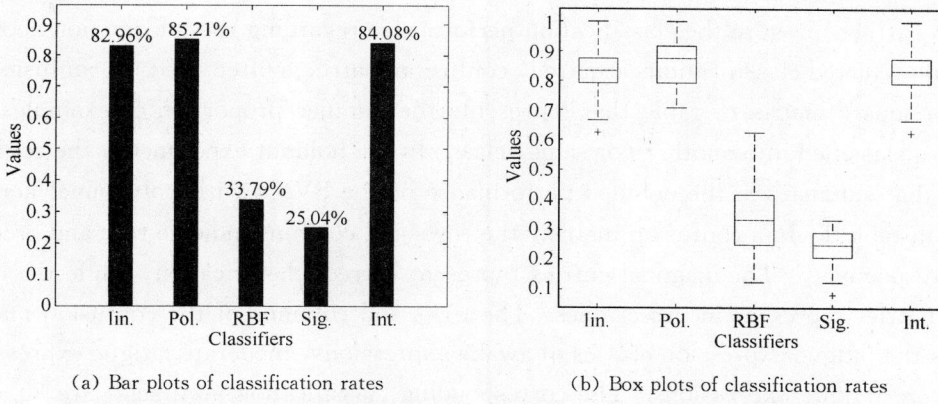

(a) Bar plots of classification rates (b) Box plots of classification rates

Fig. 5.8 Classification performance of SVMs using five kernels in holdout experiment

In the second holdout experiment, the same set of training and testing are applied to SVMs with polynomial kernel and the other four classifiers, and their classification performances are simultaneously compared. The results of classification rate for the fatigue expression are displayed in the bar plots of Fig. 5.9(a) and box plots of Fig. 5.9(b). It is obvious that SVMs with polynomial kernel offers the best performance rate among five classifiers in the second holdout experiments.

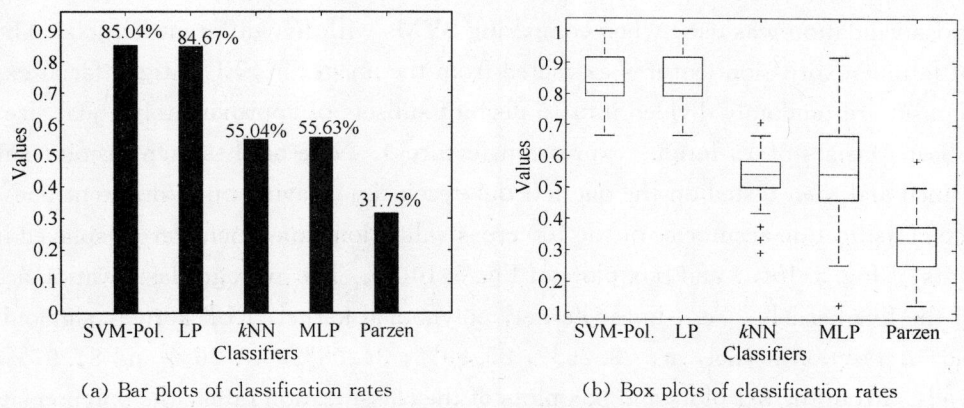

(a) Bar plots of classification rates (b) Box plots of classification rates

Fig. 5.9 Classification performance of SVMs with polynomial kernel and other four methods in holdout experiment

Table 1　Confusion matrix for the result from SVMs classifier with polynomial kernel in holdout experiments. (Ⅰ) awake expressions, (Ⅱ) moderate fatigue expressions and (Ⅲ) severe fatigue expressions.

class	Ⅰ	Ⅱ	Ⅲ
Ⅰ	80.87%	12.23%	6.90%
Ⅱ	12.29%	85.30%	2.41%
Ⅲ	13.38%	2.55%	84.08%

To further measure the classification performance regarding the information about actual and predicted classifications acquired, confusion matrix is often used. A confusion matrix is a square matrix or table that represents the number/proportion of examples from one class classified into another (or same) class. In the holdout experiment, the confusion matrix that summarizes the detailed performance of the SVMs with polynomial kernel is shown in table 1. In a confusion matrix, the rows and columns indicate true and predicted class, respectively. The diagonal entries represent correct classification, while the off-diagonal entries represent incorrect ones. The rows and columns of the confusion matrices express the fatigue expression classes of awake expressions, moderate fatigue expressions, and severe fatigue expressions. The corresponding classification accuracies are 80.87%, 85.30%, and 84.08%, respectively. From confusion matrix of the holdout experiments, it is clear that the class of moderate fatigue expression has the most recognition accuracy of three classes in the holdout experiments.

2) Cross-validation experiments

The k-fold cross validation approach is another commonly used technique that takes a set of m examples and randomly partitions them into k folds of size m/k. For each fold, the classifier is tested on one fold (consists of m/k examples) and trained on the other $k-1$ folds (consisting of $m(1-1/k)$ examples). In the first cross-validation experiment, 10-fold cross validation was used when comparing SVMs with five different kernels. The 120 sets of fatigue expression features extracted from the images in SEU fatigue facial expression dataset are randomly divided into 10 disjoint subsets of approximately equal size (every subset consists of 12 fatigue expression features). Nine of these ten disjoint subsets are trained and then tested on the one left out, each time leaving out a different one. The average classification accuracies of the 100 cross-validation experiments are displayed in the bar plots of Fig. 5.10(a) and box plots of Fig. 5.10(b). The average classification accuracies of the five kernels, i.e., linear kernel, polynomial kernel, RBF kernel, sigmoid kernel and intersection kernel, are 83.26%, 85.99%, 34.08%, 16.96% and 84.97%, respectively. From the bar plots and box plots of the classification rates, the polynomial kernel outperforms the other four kernels, because it achieves the highest classification rates among the five kernels in the first cross-validation experiments.

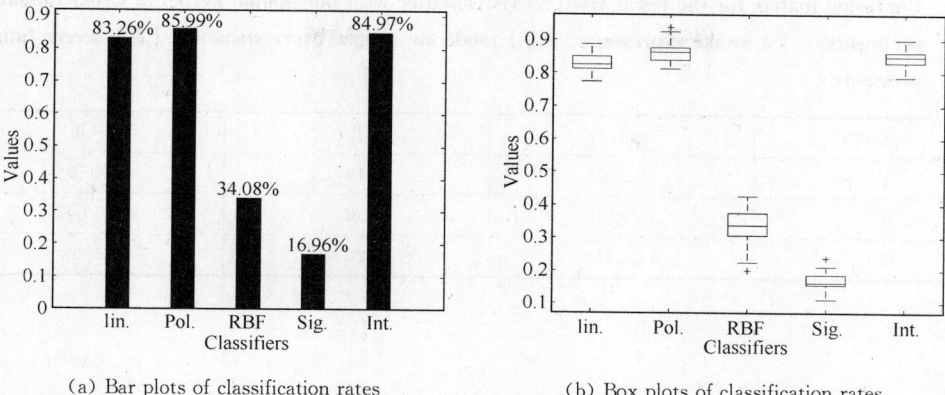

(a) Bar plots of classification rates (b) Box plots of classification rates

Fig. 5.10 Classification performance of SVMs using five kernels in Cross-validation experiment

In the second cross-validation experiment, 10-fold cross validations are applied to SVMs with polynomial kernel and the other four classifiers, and their classification performances are simultaneously compared. The results of classification rate for the fatigue expressions are displayed in the bar plots of Fig. 5.11(a) and box plots of Fig. 5.11(b). From Fig. 11, it is obvious that SVMs with polynomial kernel offers the best performance rate of five classifiers in the second cross-validation experiment. In the cross-validation experiment, the confusion matrix that summarizes the detailed performance of SVMs with polynomial kernel is shown in table 2. The accuracies of the three classes, (i.e., awake facial expression, etc.) are 85.10%, 88.60%, and 85.38%, and once again, it is clear that the class of moderate fatigue expression has the most recognition accuracy of three classes in the cross-validation experiments.

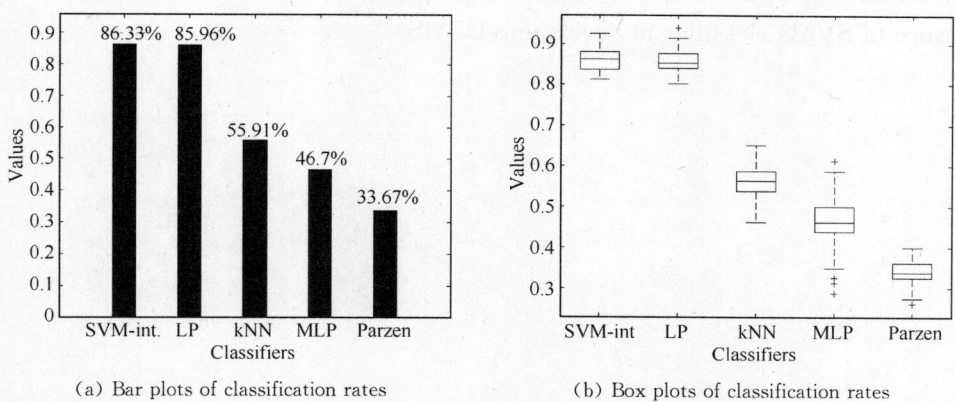

(a) Bar plots of classification rates (b) Box plots of classification rates

Fig. 5.11 Classification performance of SVMs with polynomial kernel and other four methods in Cross-validation experiment

Table 2 Confusion matrix for the result from SVMs classifier with polynomial kernel in Cross-validation experiments. （Ⅰ）awake expressions, （Ⅱ）moderate fatigue expressions and （Ⅲ）severe fatigue expressions.

class	Ⅰ	Ⅱ	Ⅲ
Ⅰ	85.10%	8.40%	6.50%
Ⅱ	10.30%	88.60%	1.09%
Ⅲ	14.42%	0.20%	85.38%

5.6 Conclusions

With features extracted by curvelet transform from SEU fatigue facial expression dataset, consisting of awake expressions, moderate fatigue expressions and severe fatigue expressions, we comparatively studied SVMs using five different kernels, with other four commonly used classification methods, namely, LP classifier, kNN classifier, MLP classifier and Parzen classifier, in the classification of three pre-defined classes of driver fatigue expressions. The holdout and cross-validation experiments were conducted, which indicated that polynomial kernel outperforms the other four kernels, and SVMs with polynomial kernel offers the best classification performance rate of five classifiers. Our experiments also showed that moderate fatigue expression has the most recognition accuracy of the three classes. With SVMs using polynomial kernel, the classification accuracies of moderate fatigue expression are over 85% in both of the holdout and cross-validation experiments, which shows the effectiveness of the proposed feature extraction method and the importance of SVMs classifier in developing DFMS.

Chapter 6
Perception of Driver's Abnormal Activities Information

A crucial step in developing image-based driving postures recognition is to extract suitable feature representation of the driver's images and characterize the differences between the different driving postures. In the paper, we proposed an efficient feature to describe a driver's postures by Nonsubsampled Contourlet Transform (NSCT), and k-Nearest Neighbour (kNN) classifier is then used to classify the features vectors into one of the four predefined classes of driving postures: grasping the steel wheel, operating the shift lever, eating a cake and talking on a cellular telephone. The rest of the paper is organized as follows.

6.1 Data acquisition and features extraction of driving postures

We designed a driving posture dataset by using a side-mounted Logitech C905 CCD camera. There are 10 female drivers and 10 male drivers in the driving postures dataset (Southeast University (SEU) dataset afterward), and the lighting conditions varied under the natural conditions, as the car was in an outdoor parking lot. The SEU driving posture dataset consists of four driving postures, i.e., grasping the steering wheel, operating the shift lever, eating a cake and talking on a cellular phone.

Fig. 6.1 shows samples of our SEU driving posture dataset consisting of 80 driving posture images, each with resolution 480×640 pixels. In order to address the problem of illumination variations in images of SEU driving postures dataset, we adopted the well-known normalization technique called Homomorphic Filter (HOMOF)[115] to enhance the image quality. With HOMOF, the images are first transformed into logarithm and then a frequency domain to emphasize the high frequency components. Then the images are transformed back into spatial domain by applying the inverse Fourier transform, followed by appropriate exponential operation. One example image of SEU driving posture dataset before and after preprocessed by HOMOF is shown in Fig. 6.2.

(a) Grasping the steering wheel (b) Operating the shift lever

(c) Eating a cake (d) Talking on a cellular phone

Fig. 6.1　Example images of SEU driving posture dataset

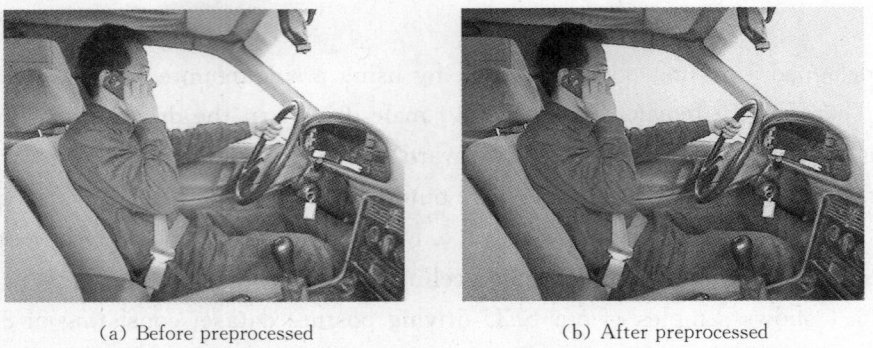

(a) Before preprocessed (b) After preprocessed

Fig. 6.2　Example image before and after preprocessed by HOMOF

　　The objects of interest in the driving images are the skin-like regions, such as the left hand, right hand and driver's head. It is a fact that human skin tones have very similar chromatic properties regardless of race, and skin colour detection can be fairly robust under certain illumination conditions. The classification of colour pixels into non-skin tones and skin tones can be performed by working in the normalized RGB space. An RGB triplet (r, g, b) with values for each primary colour between 0 and 255 is normalized into the triplet (r', g', b') by using the following relationships:

$$r' = \frac{255r}{r+g+b}, \quad g' = \frac{255g}{r+g+b}, \quad b' = \frac{255b}{r+g+b} \tag{6-1}$$

The normalized colour (r', g', b') is classified as a skin colour if it lies within the region of the normalized RGB space described by the following rules.

$$\begin{cases} r' > 95, \quad g' > 45, \quad b' > 20 \\ \max\{r', g', b'\} - \min\{r', g', b'\} > 15 \\ r' - g' > 15, \quad r' > b' \end{cases} \tag{6-2}$$

Fig. 6.3 shows the skin-colour segmentation results of the four example images preprocessed by HOMOF.

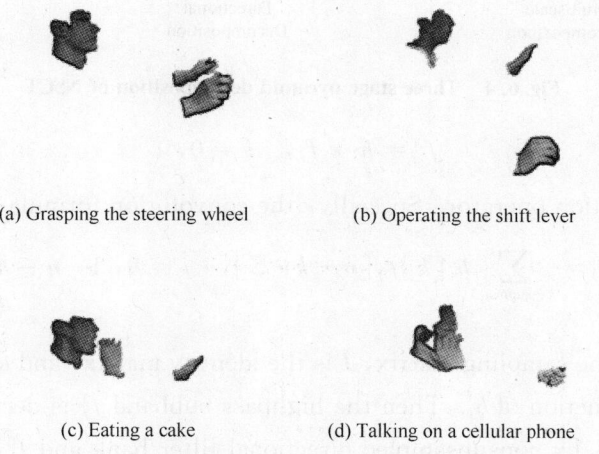

(a) Grasping the steering wheel (b) Operating the shift lever

(c) Eating a cake (d) Talking on a cellular phone

Fig. 6.3 Skin-colour segmentation preprocessed by HOMOF.

6.2 Features extraction by Nonsubsampled Contourlet Transform (NSCT)

The Nonsubsampled Contourlet Transform (NSCT)[164], which allows redundancy, is a new development of contourlet transform. Allowing redundancy would make NSCT represent images more completely and more flexibly, and Fig. 6.4 illustrates an overview of NSCT.

NSCT is implemented by nonsubsampled filter bank structures. More specifically, it is constructed by combining the nonsubsampled pyramid structure that ensures the multi-scale property and the nonsubsampled directional filter bank structure that gives varying directions. Denote f_j as the input signal in the jth level ($1 \leqslant j \leqslant J$). Nonsubsampled pyramid first splits f_j into a high-pass subband f_j^1 and a lowpass subband f_j^0 using high-pass filter h_1 and low-pass filter h_0:

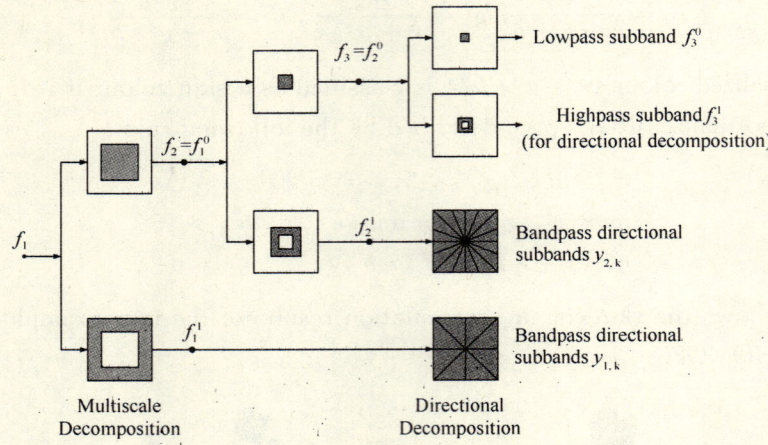

Fig. 6.4 Three-stage pyramid decomposition of NSCT

$$f_j^i = h_i * f_j, \quad i = 0, 1 \tag{6-3}$$

where $*$ is convolution operator. Specially, the convolution formula is

$$f_j^i[n] = \sum_{k \in \operatorname{supp}(h_i)} h_i[k] f_j[n - k \cdot S], \quad i = 0, 1 \quad n \in N \times N \tag{6-4}$$

where $S = 2^{j-1} I$ is the sampling matrix, I is the identity matrix, and $\operatorname{supp}(h_i)$ is the compactly supported function of h_i. Then the highpass subband f_j^1 is decomposed into several directional subbands by nonsubsampled directional filter bank and f_j^0 is for the next-stage decomposition. The nonsubsampled directional filter bank is constructed in cascade by combining two-channel fan filter banks and parallelogram filters without upsamplers and downsamplers. Consequently, the number of the directional subbands at a specific level is a power of two. We denote the equivalent filter for the k-th direction as u_k^{eq}, then the directional subbands can be obtained by

$$y_{j,k} = u_k^{eq} * f_j^1, \quad k = 1, \cdots, 2^{l_j} \tag{6-5}$$

where 2^{l_j} is the number of directional subbands at the j-th level. This procedure would repeat on the low-pass subband by setting $f_{j+1} = f_j^0$ for the next level decomposition and the final low-pass subband is f_j^0, so that directional subbands of different levels are generated. For the next level, all filters of pyramid are upsampled by 2 in both dimensions and this operation has been implied in the Eq. (6-4). It should be noted that filtering with the upsampled filters does not increase computational complexity. In this paper, the "dmaxflat7" filters and the "maxflat" filters are, respectively, selected for nonsubsampled directional and nonsubsampled pyramid filter bank.

The reconstruction of NSCT is also based on filtering operation according to the invert procedure of decomposition. Assume g_0 and g_1 are the corresponding synthesis filters of h_0 and h_1, respectively, and v_k^{eq} is the synthesis filter of u_k^{eq}. Then reconstruction of NSCT can be described as follows:

$$\begin{cases} \hat{f}_j^0 = \hat{f}_{j+1} \\ \hat{f}_j^1 = \sum_{k=1}^{2^{l_j}} v_k^{eq} * y_{j,k} \quad j = 1, \cdots, J \\ \hat{f}_j = g_0 * \hat{f}_j^0 + g_1 * \hat{f}_j^1 \end{cases} \quad (6\text{-}6)$$

Given directional subbands $\{y_{j,k}\}_{j,k}$ and the low-pass subband f_j^0, by setting $\hat{f}_{j+1} = f_j^0$ and iterating the procedure in Eq. (6-6) from the J-th level to the first level, the input signal can be reconstructed by $\hat{f} = \hat{f}_1$. NSCT differs from other multi-scale analysis methods in which the contourlet transform allows for different and flexible number of directions at each scale. According to the direction information, directional filter bank can concatenate the neighboring singular points into (local) contours in the frequency domain, and therefore the detection of contours is obtained. By combination of nonsubsampled directional and nonsubsampled pyramid filter bank, NSCT is constructed as a fully shift-invariant, multi-scale and multi-direction decomposition. One example image decomposed into 3 levels by nonsubsampled contourlet transform is shown in Fig. 6.5, and the coefficients of lowpass subband f_3^0 are used as the features of the driving postures in the following experiments.

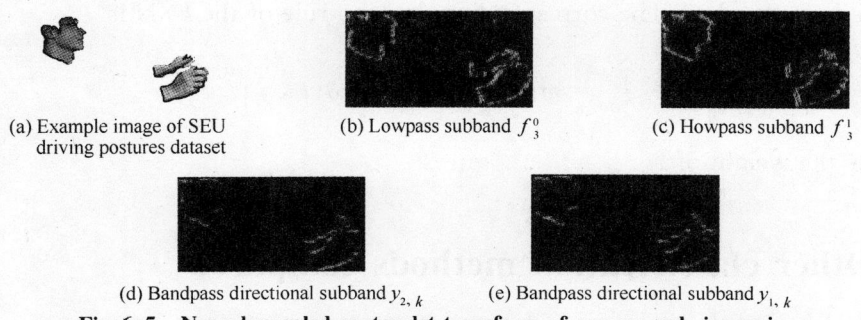

(a) Example image of SEU driving postures dataset
(b) Lowpass subband f_3^0
(c) Howpass subband f_3^1
(d) Bandpass directional subband $y_{2,k}$
(e) Bandpass directional subband $y_{1,k}$

Fig. 6.5 Nonsubsampled contourlet transform of one example image in SEU driving postures dataset.

6.3 *k*-Nearest Neighbor (*k*NN) classifier

In pattern recognition, k-Nearest Neighbor (kNN) is a method for classifying objects based on closest training examples in the feature space[165]. Let $X = [x_1, \cdots, x_N]$ be the training data with N points of dimensionality D, and $X_i = [x_{i1}, \cdots, x_{ik}]$ be the k nearest neighbors of x_i. The testing data are denoted as X_t with N_t points. x_0 is an arbitrary testing data point, and $X_0 = [x_{01}, \cdots, x_{0k}]$ contains its k nearest neighbors from training data, with labels denoted as $[l_1, \cdots, l_k]$. Suppose there are C classes in the data denoted as $\Omega = [\Omega_1, \cdots, \Omega_C]$. The kNN classifier finds the k nearest neighbors of a testing point in the training data and assigns the testing point to the most frequently occurring class of its k neighbors. The kNN classifies x_0 with the following majority voting rule:

$$j^* = \arg \max_{j=1,\cdots,C} \sum_{i=1}^{k} \delta(l_i, j) \tag{6-7}$$

where δ is the Kronecker delta, and satisfies

$$\delta(l_i, j) = \begin{cases} 1 & \text{if } l_i = j \\ 0 & \text{otherwise} \end{cases} \tag{6-8}$$

The kNN classification can potentially be improved by learning a distance metric derived from the training data, e.g.,

$$dis(x_i, x_j) = \| T(x_i - x_j) \|^2 \tag{6-9}$$

where T represents a linear transformation[166]. Because nonlinear dimensionality reduction is associated with some transformation of the original data, it can also be regarded as an approach to obtain a new distance metric. In kNN, the k neighbors of a testing point are assumed to have equal weights. It is appealing to assign different weights to the neighbors and then classify the testing point as the class for which the weights set to its neighbors sum to the largest value. The corresponding decision rule of the kNN is

$$j^* = \arg \max_{j=1,\cdots,C} \sum_{i=1}^{k} \omega_i \cdot \delta(l_i, j) \tag{6-10}$$

where w_i is the weight of x_{0i}.

6.4 Other classification methods compared

1) Intersection Kernel Support Vector Machine (IKSVM)

Support vector machines (SVMs) were originally designed for binary-class classification problems, based on the idea of structural risk minimization. The basic principle of binary-class SVMs is to find an Optimal Separating Hyperplane (OSH) and separate two classes of patterns based on the training set and the decision boundary, which can be formulated as a Quadratic Programming (QP) problem in the feature space. A variety of schemes have been proposed in the literature for solving multi-class problem by using techniques including one-against-all strategy, one-against-one strategy, and multiclass objective function by adding bias to the objective function. Tuning the hyperparameters of a

SVM classifier is a crucial step in order to establish an efficient classification system. Generally, at least two parameter values have to be chosen carefully in advance. They concern respectively the regularization parameter C, which sets the trade-off cost between the training error and the complexity of the model, and the kernel function parameter, reduced to the bandwidth in the classical case of a radial basis function kernel.

The problem of choosing these parameters values is called model selection in the literature and its results strongly impact the performance of the classifier. In this paper, we followed the conventional grid search method which selects the parameters empirically by trying a finite number of values and keeping those that provide the least test error. The histogram intersection kernel, $k_{HI}(h_a, h_b) = \sum_{i=1}^{n} \text{expmin}(h_a(i), h_b(i))$ has been used as a measurement of similarity between histograms h_a and h_b. Due to the positive definite property, it can be used as a kernel for discriminative classification using SVMs. Recently, IKSVM has been shown to be successful for a number of tasks, for instance, detection and recognition. However, the earlier successful application of IKSVM often comes at great computational cost compared to simpler linear SVMs, because non-linear kernels require memory and computation linearly proportional to the number of support vectors for classification. Recently Maji et al proposed a fast IKSVM[157] with an approximation scheme whose time and space complexity is $O(n)$, independent of the number of support vectors. The key idea is that for a class of kernels including the intersection kernel, the classifier can be decomposed as a sum of functions, one for each histogram bin, each of which can be efficiently computed.

2) Multilayer Perception (MLP) classifier

Multilayer Perception (MLP) classifier is a modification of the standard linear perceptron, which can distinguish data that is not linearly separable. A multilayer perceptron is a feedforward artificial neural network model that maps sets of input data onto a set of appropriate output, and consists of a set of source nodes forming the input layer, one or more hidden layers of computation nodes, and an output layer of nodes[162]. The MLP utilizes a supervised learning technique called backpropagation for training the network and constructs input-output mappings that are a nested composition of nonlinearities with the form

$$y = f(\sum g(\sum (\cdot))) \tag{6-11}$$

where the number of function compositions is given by the number of network layers. An MLP can be trained by gradient descent using the back-propagation algorithm to optimize any derivable criterion, such as the Mean Squared Error, here, an MLP is trained to classify an input to be one of the given class labels. The input of the MLP is a vector corresponding to the features extracted from gait patterns. The output of the MLP is either 1 (if the input corresponds to a control group) or -1 (if the input corresponds to children with CP). Though MLPs have been proved to be able to virtually approximate any function with any desired accuracy, there is a common criticism for MLP that is very difficult to interpret the trained discriminant function.

3) Parzen classifier

Parzen classifier is a kernel density estimator, with which a nonlinear function is approximated by the superposition of a set of kernels. For pattern x_j, a Gaussian kernel-based Parzen classifier is determined by N training samples $X = [X_1, X_2, \cdots, X_N]$ as follows:

$$f(\pmb{x}_j, s) = \frac{1}{N} \sum_{i=1}^{N} \frac{1}{(s\sqrt{2\pi})^n} \exp\left(-\frac{\|\pmb{x}_j - \pmb{x}_i\|^2}{2s^2}\right) \tag{6-12}$$

where $\pmb{x}_i$ is an n-dimensions training feature vector of training sample X_i, and s is a kernel width. The Parzen classifier design means to estimate the relevant kernel width s using the training feature set $\{\pmb{x}_1, \cdots, \pmb{x}_i, \cdots, \pmb{x}_N\}$. A maximum likelihood principle proposed by Kraaijveld[163] was adopted to estimate the kernel width s which is as follows:

$$s = \sqrt{\frac{1}{n \cdot N} \sum_{j=1}^{N} \sum_{i \neq j}^{N} \frac{\|\pmb{x}_j - \pmb{x}_i\|^2}{N-1}} \tag{6-13}$$

6.5 Experimental results

Two standard experimental procedures, namely the holdout approach and the cross-validation approach, are used to compare the performance of proposed features extraction method and kNN classifier, compared with other three classifiers, namely, IKSVM, MLP classifier and Parzen classifier. In the holdout approach, certain amounts of features extracted by NSCT from SEU driving postures dataset (shown in Fig. 6.6) are reserved for testing, and the rest are for training.

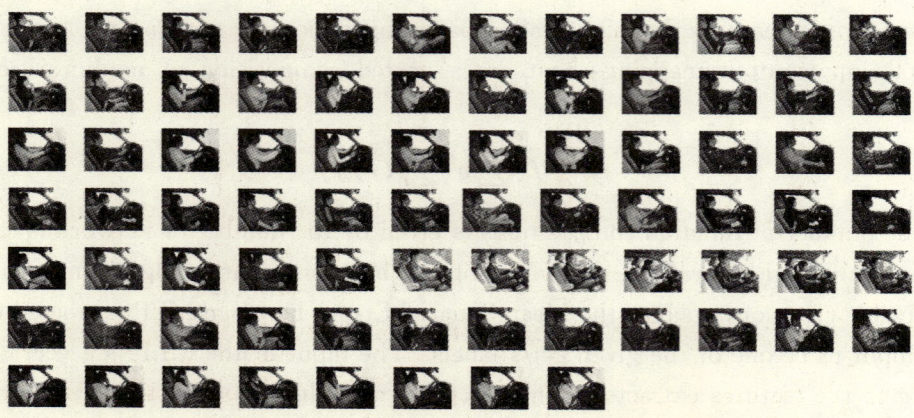

Fig. 6.6 **SEU driving postures dataset**

In k-fold cross-validation approach, the driving posture datasets are partitioned into k sub-datasets. Of them, the kth sub-dataset is retained for testing the classification model, and the remaining $k-1$ sub-datasets are used for training the classification model. The cross-validation experiments are then repeated k times, with all of the k sub-samples used exactly once as the validation dataset[163]. The k experiment results from the folds are then averaged to produce a single classification rate.

1) Holdout experiments

Holdout experiments are based on randomly dividing driving posture features into a training dataset (80% of driving postures features extracted from the images in the SEU driving posture dataset) and a test dataset (20% of driving postures features extracted from the images in the SEU driving posture dataset). Using the holdout experiment approach, only the test dataset is used to estimate the generalization error. We repeated the holdout experiment 100 times by randomly splitting the driving posture datasets, and recorded the classification results. For each random testing, the same set of training and testing are applied to the four classifiers and their classification performances are simultaneously compared.

The classification rate is first simple performance indicator for a classifier accuracy. The results of classification rate for the driving postures are displayed in the bar plots of Fig. 6.7 (a) and box plots of Fig. 6.7 (b), which are the averaged classification results from the 100 random splits of the driving posture dataset into training and testing sets. The average classification accuracies of IKSVM, MLP classifier, Parzen classifier, and kNN classifier, are 70.5%, 33.25%, 70.94%, and 88.06%, respectively. From Fig. 6.7, it is obvious that kNN classifier offers the best performance of the three classifiers in the holdout experiments.

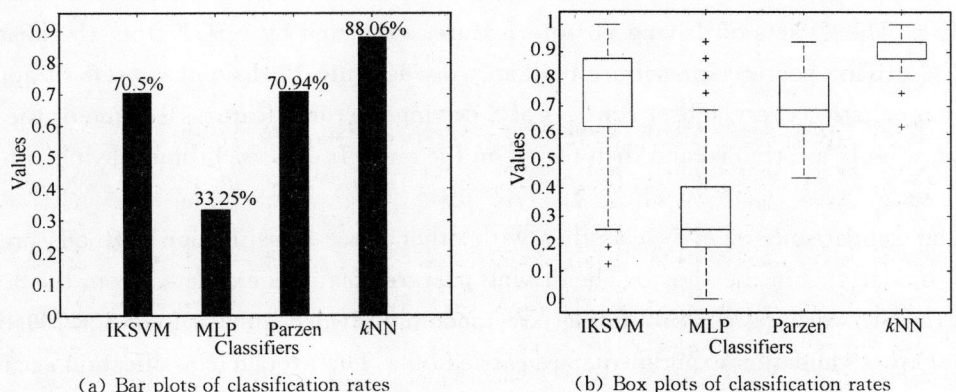

(a) Bar plots of classification rates (b) Box plots of classification rates

Fig. 6.7 Classification performance of four classifiers in holdout experiments

To further measure the classification performance regarding the information about actual and predicted classifications acquired, confusion matrix is often used. A confusion matrix is a square matrix or table that represents the number/proportion of examples from one class classified into another (or same) class. In the holdout experiments, the confusion matrix that summarizes the detailed performance of kNN, is shown in table 6.1. In a confusion matrix, the rows and columns indicate true and predicted class, respectively. The diagonal entries represent correct classification, while the off-diagonal entries represent incorrect ones. The rows and columns of the confusion matrices express the posture classes of grasping the steering wheel, operating the shift gear, eating a cake and talking on a cellular phone. The corresponding classification accuracies are 99.76%, 88.46%, 77.89% and 86.34%, respectively. From the confusion matrix of the holdout experiments, it is clear that of the four classes, eating a cake is the most difficult to classify.

Table 6.1 Confusion matrix for the result from kNN classifier in the holdout experiments. (Ⅰ) grasping the steering wheel, (Ⅱ) operating the shift lever, (Ⅲ) eating a cake and (Ⅳ) talking on a cellular phone.

class	Ⅰ	Ⅱ	Ⅲ	Ⅳ
Ⅰ	99.76%	0.24%	0	0
Ⅱ	8.72%	88.46%	2.05%	0.77%
Ⅲ	0	0.75%	77.89%	21.36%
Ⅳ	0	0	13.66%	86.34%

2) Cross-validation experiments

The k-fold cross validation approach is another commonly used technique that takes a set of m examples and randomly partitions them into k folds of size m/k. For each fold, the classifier is tested on one fold (consists of m/k examples) and trained on the other $k-1$ folds (consisting of $m(1-1/k)$ examples). In the following experiments, 10-fold cross validation was used when comparing IKSVM, MLP classifier, Parzen classifier and kNN classifier. The 80 sets of driving posture features extracted by NSCT from the images in the SEU driving posture dataset are randomly divided into 10 disjoint subsets of approximately equal size (every subset consists of 8 driving postures features). Nine of these ten disjoint subsets are trained and then tested on the one left out, each time leaving out a different one.

The comparisons of kNN classifier with other three classification methods are processed similarly as in the above. The driving postures features extracted from the 80 images in the SEU driving posture dataset are randomly divided into 10 folds for 100 times, and 100 cross-validation experiments are carried out. The average classification accuracies of the 100 cross-validation experiments are displayed in the bar plots of Fig. 6.8 (a) and box plots of Fig. 6.8 (b). The average classification accuracies of IKSVM, MLP classifier, Parzen classifier and kNN classifier, are 75.29%, 30.11%, 68.06%, and 88.25%, respectively. From the bar plots and box plots of the classification rates, kNN classifier outperforms the other three classifiers, because it achieves the highest classification rates among the four classifiers in the cross-validation experiments.

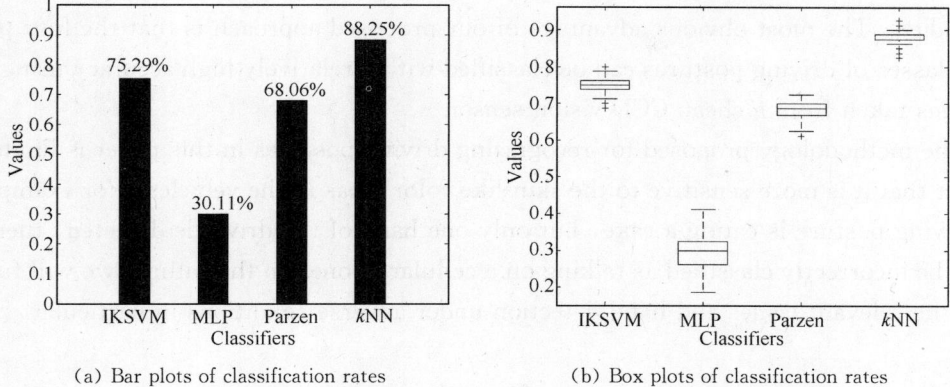

(a) Bar plots of classification rates (b) Box plots of classification rates

Fig. 6.8 Classification performance of four classifiers in cross-validation experiments

In the cross-validation experiment, the confusion matrix that summarizes the detailed performance of kNN classifier is shown in table 6.2. The accuracies of the four classes, (i.e., grasping the steering wheel, etc.) are 99.79%, 88.24%, 78.22% and 89.65%, and once again, it is clear that eating a cake is the most difficult posture to classify of the four classes in the cross-validation experiments.

Table 6.2 Confusion matrix for the result from kNN classifier in the cross-validation experiments. (I) grasping the steering wheel, (II) operating the shift lever, (III) eating a cake and (IV) talking on a cellular phone.

class	I	II	III	IV
I	99.79%	0.16%	0	0.04%
II	9.31%	88.24%	2.44%	0
III	0	1.42%	78.22%	20.36%
IV	0	0	10.35%	89.65%

3) Discussions

Compared to other state of the art methodologies for monitoring driver's behaviours in current research literature[148], three contributions are presented in this paper. With the potential for flexible multiscale, multidirection and shift-invariant image decomposition, the Nonsubsampled Contourlet Transform (NSCT) has the good ability for feature description of driving posture images. The first contribution of this paper is that we proposed an effective feature extraction approach for driving postures using NSCT. The second contribution is that kNN classifier compared with IKSVM, MLP classifier and Parzen classifier, is exploited in classifying four pre-defined classes of driving postures. The third contribution is our empirical proof of the effectiveness of the proposed feature extraction method and kNN classifier in the recognition of driving postures. Some special issues have been identified from the experiments. Particularly we showed that eating a cake is the most difficult situation to be automatically recognized among the four driving posture classes studied. The most obvious advantage of our proposed approach is that the four predefined classes of driving postures can be classified with a relatively high accuracy using static images taken from a cheap CCD vision sensor.

The methodology proposed for recognizing driving postures in this paper is limited by the fact that it is more sensitive to the skin-like color areas in the vehicles. For example, if the driving posture is eating a cake, but only one hand of the driver is detected, then this would be incorrectly classified as talking on a cellular phone. In the future, we will further study the relevant issues and hand detection under adverse conditions in particular.

6.6 Conclusions

To automatically understand and characterize the driver's behaviours, four different pattern classification paradigms are studied in the automatically understanding and characterizing driver's behaviours. With features extracted by NSCT from a driving posture dataset consisting of grasping the steering wheel, operating the shift lever, eating a cake and talking on a cellular phone, created at Southeast University, we comparatively studied kNN classifier with other three commonly used classification methods, including IKSVM, MLP classifier, and Parzen classifier, in the classification of four pre-defined classes of driving postures. With the features extracted by NSCT, the holdout and cross-validation experiments were conducted, which indicated that kNN classifier outperforms the other three classifiers. Our experiments also showed that eating a cake is the most difficult one among the four classes studied. With the proposed features extraction method and kNN classifier, the classification accuracies of eating a cake are over 88% in both of the holdout and cross-validation experiments, which shows the effectiveness of the proposed feature extraction method and the importance of kNN classifier in automatically understanding and characterizing driver's behaviours towards human-centric driver assistance systems.

参考文献

[1] Sun Z, Bebis G, Miller R. On-road vehicle detection: a review [J]. IEEE Transactions on Pattern Analysis and Machine Intelligence, 2006, 28(5):694-711.

[2] Gupte S, Masoud O, Martin R F K, et al. Detection and classification of vehicles [J]. IEEE Transactions on Intelligent Transportation Systems, 2002, 3 (1):37-47.

[3] Foresti G L, Murino V, Regazzoni C. Vehicle Recognition and Tracking from Road Image Sequences [J]. IEEE Transactions on Vehicular Technology, 1999, 48(1):301-318.

[4] Gao L, Li C, Fang T, et al. Vehicle detection based on color and edge information [J]. Lecture Notes in Computer Science, 2008(5112):142-150.

[5] Guo D, Fraichard T, Xie M, et al. Color modeling by spherical influence field in sensing driving environment [C]. Intelligent Vehicles Symposium, 2000:249-254.

[6] Techawatcharapaikul C, Kaewtrakulpong P, Siddhichai S. Outdoor vehicle and shadow segmentation by temporal edge density information of adjacent frames [J]. Telecommunications and Information Technology, 2008, 1(3):433-436.

[7] Johansson B, Wiklund J, Forssén P, et al. Combining shadow detection and simulation for estimation of vehicle size and position [J]. Pattern Recognition Letters, 2009, 30(8):751-759.

[8] Cucchiara R, Piccardi M. Vehicle Detection under Day and Night Illumination [C]. International Conference on Networking, Sensing and Control, 1999.

[9] Nikul U, Mehta H. An accurate method for license plate localization using morphological operations and edge processing [J]. Image and Signal Processing, 2010, 5(12):2488-2491.

[10] Zheng D, Zhao Y, Wang J. An efficient method of license plate location [J]. Pattern Recognition Letters, 2005, 26(15):2431-2438.

[11] Kalinke T, Tzomakas C, von Seelen W. A texture based object detection and an adaptive model-based classification [J]. IEEE Intelligent Vehicles Symposium, 1998:341-346.

[12] Kim K J, Park S M, Baek N. A texture-Based algorithm for vehicle area segmentation using the support vector machine Method [J]. Lecture Notes in Computer Science, 2007(4482):542-549.

[13] Wu J, Zhang X, Zhou J. Vehicle detection in static road images with PCA and wavelet based classifier [C]. IEEE Conference on Intelligent Transportation Systems, 2001:742-746.

[14] Sun Z, Bebis G, Miller R. On-road vehicle detection using Gabor filters and support vector machines [C]. Greece: International Conference on Digital Signal Processing, 2002:1019-1022.

[15] Zielke T, Brauckmann M, Seelen W V. Intensity and edge-based symmetry detection with an application to car-following [J]. Image Understanding, 1993, 58(2):177-190.

[16] Du Y, Papanikolopoulos N P. Real-time vehicle following through a novel symmetry-based approach [J]. IEEE International Conference on Robotics and Automation, 1997, 4:3160-3165.

[17] Bin D, Yajun F, Tao W. A vehicle detection method via symmetry in multi-scale windows[C]. IEEE Conference on Industrial Electronics and Applications, 2007:1827-1831.

[18] Teoh S S, Bräunl T. Symmetry-based monocular vehicle detection system [J]. Machine Vision and Applications, 2012, 23(5):831-842.

[19] Viola P, Jones M. Robust Real-time Object Detection [J]. International Journal of Computer Vision, 2004, 57(2):137-154.

[20] Dalal N, Triggs B. Histogram of oriented gradients for human detection [C]. IEEE Computer Society Conference on Computer Vision and Pattern Recognition. Montbonnot, France, 2005, 1:886-893.

[21] Chang C, Wang C, Lien J. Multi-view vehicle detection using gentle boost with sharing hog features [C]. Taiwan: 22th IPPR Conference on Computer Vision, Graphics and Image Processing, 2009: 1688-1694.

[22] Ferryman J, Worral A, Sulliva G, et al. A generic deformable model for vehicle recognition [C]. British Machine Vision Conference, 1995:127-136.

[23] Wei W, Zhang Q, Wang M. A method of vehicle classification using models and neural networks[C]. IEEE Vehicular Technology Conference, 2001.

[24] Petrović V, Cootes T. Analysis of features for rigid structure vehicle type recognition [C]. British Machine Vision Conference, 2004.

[25] Petrović V, Cootes T. Vehicle type recognition with match refinement [C]. International Conference on Pattern Recognition, 2004:95-98.

[26] Munroe D T, Madden M G. Multi-class and single-class classification approaches to vehicle Model recognition from images[C]. Portstewart: Irish Conference on Artificial Intelligence and Cognitive Science, 2005.

[27] Dlagnekov L. Video-based car surveillance: License plate make and model recognition [D]. San Diego: University of California, 2005.

[28] Zafar I, Edirisinghe E A, Acar B S. Vehicle make & model identification using scale invariant transforms [C]. The 7th IASTED International Conference on Visualization, Imaging and Image Processing, 2007:271-276.

[29] Lowe D G. Distinctive image features from scale-invariant keypoints [J]. International Journal of Computer Vision, 2004, 60(2):91-110.

[30] Anthony D. More local structure information for Make-Model Recognition [D]. San Diego: Department of Computer Science, University of California, taken from http://www-cse.ucsd.edu.

[31] Zafar I, Edirisinghe E A, Acar B S, et al. Two dimensional statistical linear discriminant analysis for real-time robust vehicle type recognition[C]. International Conference on Real-Time Image Processing, 2007, 6496:1-8.

[32] Li M, Yuan B. 2D-LDA: A statistical linear discriminant analysis for image matrix [J]. Pattern Recognition Letters, 2005, 26(5):527-532.

[33] Kazemi F, Samadi S, Pourreza H, et al. Vehicle recognition based on fourier, wavelet and curvelet transforms—a comparative study [C]. The 4th International Conference on Information Technology, Mashad, 2007:939-940.

[34] Rahati S, Moravejian R, Kazemi E M, et al. Vehicle recognition using contourlet transform and SVM

[C]. The 5th IEEE International Conference on Information Technology: New Generations, 2008: 894-898.

[35] Zafar I, Edirisinghe E A, Acar B S. Localized contourlet features in vehicle make and model recognition[J]. In Proceedings SPIE, Electronic Imaging, 2009, 7251:1-6.

[36] Negri P. An Oriented-Contour Point Based Voting Algorithm for Vehicle Type Classification[C]. The 18th International Conference on Pattern Recognition, 2006:574-577.

[37] Zhang B. Reliable Classification of Vehicle Types Based on Cascade Classifier Ensembles [J]. IEEE Transactions on Intelligent Transportation Systems, 2013, 14(1):322-332.

[38] 杨文强,吴冰,陈步威. 基于特征匹配算法的车型识别研究[J]. 信息通信,2008,(4):73-75.

[39] 季晨光,张晓宇,白相宇. 基于视频图像中的车型识别[J]. 辽宁工业大学学报,2010,30(1):5-7.

[40] 王枚,王国宏,于元港,等. 新车型识别方法及其在套牌车辆鉴别中的应用[J]. 计算机工程与应用, 2009, 45(17):211-214.

[41] 姚源. 车辆图像的特征提取[D]. 长沙:中南大学,2008.

[42] 马蓓,张乐. 基于纹理特征的汽车车型识别[J]. 图像编码与软件,2010, 23(2):94-97.

[43] 何得平,朱光喜,赵广州. 快速 Gabor 滤波器在车型识别中的应用[J]. 计算机应用, 2008(12):193-195.

[44] 赵英男,刘正东,杨静宇. 一种基于 Gabor 滤波器的车型识别方法[J]. 计算机工程,2005, 31(22): 172-174.

[45] Do M, Vetterli M. Contourlets. A directional multiresolution image representation [C]. New York: International Conference on Image Processing, 2002:357-360.

[46] Cortes C, Vapnik V. Support-Vector Networks [J]. Machine Learning, 1995, 20(3):273-2979.

[47] Haykin S. Neural Networks. A Comprehensive Foundation [M]. 2nd edition. NJ: Prentice-Hall, 1998.

[48] Breiman L. Bagging predictors [J]. Machine Learning. 1996, 24:123-140.

[49] Freund Y, Schapire R. A decision-theoretic generalization of on-line learning and an application to boosting [J]. Computational Learning Theory Lecture Notes in Computer Science, 1997,55:119-139.

[50] Breiman L. Random forests [J]. Machine Learning, 2001, 45(1):5-32.

[51] Kuncheva L, Rodriguez J, Plumpton C, et al. Random subspace ensembles for fMRI classification [J]. IEEE Transactions on Medical Imaging, 2010 ,29(2):531-542.

[52] Chow C K. On optimum recognition error and reject tradeoff [J]. IEEE Transactions on Information Theory, 1970,16(1):41-46.

[53] Giusti N, Masulli F, Sperduti A. A theoretical and experimental analysis of a two-stage system for classification [J]. IEEE Transactions on Pattern Analysis and Machine Intelligence, 2002, 24(7):893-904.

[54] Zhang P, Bui T D, Suen C Y. A novel cascade ensemble classifier system with a high recognition performance on handwritten digits [J]. Pattern Recognition, 2007, 40(12):3415-3429.

[55] Jitprasithsiri S, Lee H, Robert G. Development of a New Digital Pavement Image Processing Algorithm for Unified Crack Index Computation[C]. A Dissertation Submitted to the Faculty of the University of Utah, 1997:142-148.

[56] Sun Y, Salar E I and Chou E. Automated Pavement Distress Detection Using Advanced Image Processing Techniques[C]. IEEE International Conference on Electro/Information Technology, 2009: 373-377.

[57] 孙波成,邱延峻. 路面裂缝图像处理算法研究[J]. 公路交通科技,2008,25(2):64-68.

[58] Koutsopoulos H N, Downey A B. Primitive-based Classification of Pavement Cracking Images[J]. Journal of Transportation Engineering,1993,19(3):13-143.

[59] Chou J, Neill O, Cheng H. Pavement Distress Evaluation Using Fuzzy Logic and Moment Invariants[J]. Transportation Research Record,1995,1505:39-46.

[60] Cheng H, Chen J, Glazier C, et al. Novel Approach to Pavement Cracking Detection Based on Fuzzy Set Theory[J]. Journal of Computing in Civil Engineering,1999,13(4):270-280.

[61] Li G, Tong Y, Xiao X. Adaptive Fuzzy Enhancement Algorithm of Surface Image based on Local Discrimination via Grey Entropy[J]. Advanced in Control Engineering and Information Science,2011,15:1590-1594.

[62] 郭宝良. CCD图像处理及算法在沥青路面破损检测中的研究[D]. 济南:山东理工大学,2011.

[63] 欧阳琰. 道路信息自动检查中的路面破损识别方法及其实现研究[D]. 武汉:武汉理工大学,2009.

[64] Cheng H. Automated Real-time Pavement Distress Detection Using Fuzzy Logic and Neural Network[C]. SPIE Proceeding,1996:140-151.

[65] Nejad F M, Zakeri H. An optimum feature extraction method based on Wavelet-Radon Transform and Dynamic Neural Network for pavement distress classification[J]. Expert Systems with Applications,2011,38(9):9442-9460.

[66] 陈利利. 基于多尺度图像分析的路面病害检测方法研究与分析[D]. 南京:南京理工大学,2009.

[67] Wang X, Feng X. Pavement distress detection and classification with automated image processing[C]. 2011 International Conference on Transportation, Mechanical, and Electrical Engineering,2011:1345-1350.

[68] Wu C, Lu B, Chen D, et al. Pavement Image Denoising Based on Shearlet Transform[C]. 2011 International Conference on Electronics and Optoelectronics,2011:262-265.

[69] 李刚. 基于图像工程的路面破损自动识别算法研究[D]. 西安:长安大学,2010.

[70] 胡士昆. 基于数字图像处理技术的路面裂缝算法研究[D]. 南京:南京邮电大学,2012,2.

[71] 吕岩,曲仕茹. 基于Beamlet变换的路面裂缝图像匀光算法[J]. 交通运输系统工程与信息,2011,11(5):123-128.

[72] 董立文,贾朱植,谢元旦,等. 一种基于小波变换的图像去噪方法[J]. 鞍山科技大学学报,2004,27(3):212-215.

[73] Huang Y, Xu B. Automatic Inspection of Pavement Cracking Distress[J]. Journal of Electronic Imaging,2006,15(1):92-98.

[74] Li L, Chan P, Rao A, et al. Flexible Pavement Distress Evaluation Using Image Analysis[J]. Journal of Transportation Engineering,1993,119(3):402-418.

[75] Grivas D A, Bhagvati C, Skolnick M M, et al. Feasibility of Automating Pavement Distress Assessment Using Mathematical Morphology[J]. Transportation Research,1994,1435(8):52-58.

[76] Yan M, Bo S, Xu K. Pavement Crack Detection and Analysis for High-grade Highway[C]. The Eighth International Conference on Electronic Measurement and Instruments,2007:548-552.

[77] 冯永安,刘万军. 边缘检测改进算法在路面破损检测中的应用[J]. 辽宁工程技术大学学报,2007,26(Suppl):176-178.

[78] 李莉,孙立军,陈长. 适于路面破损图像处理的边缘检测方法[J]. 同济大学学报,2011,39(5):688-692.

[79] 李晋惠. 用图像处理的方法检测公路路面裂缝类病害[J]. 长安大学学报(自然科学版),2004,24(3):

24-29.

[80] 唐磊,赵春霞,王鸿南,等.基于图像分析的路面裂缝检测和分类[J].工程图学学报,2008,3:99-104.

[81] Huo X, Chen J, and Donoho D L. Multiscale detection of filamentary features in image data[J]. Wavelets: Applications in Signal and Image Processing, 2003:592-606.

[82] Kumar A, Pang G K H. Defect detection in textured materials using Gabor filters[J]. IEEE Transaction on Industry Apprications, 2002, 38(2):425-440.

[83] 张雷,马建,宋宏勋.小波域内基于块的路面破损检测算法[J].郑州大学学报,2009,30(3):48-51.

[84] 李刚,贺昱曜,赵妍.基于大津法和互信息量的路面破损图像自动识别算法[J].微电子学与计算机,2009,26(7):241-243.

[85] 赵吉广.基于视频图像的路面性能参数采集方法研究[D].南京:东南大学,2006.

[86] Zhang H G, Wang Q. Use of Artificial Living System for Pavement Distress Survey[C]. The 30th Annual Conference of the IEEE Industrial Electronics Society, 2004:2486-2490.

[87] Haralick R M, Bosley R. Texture features for image classification[J]. IEEE Transactions on Systems, Man and Cybernetics, 1973, 3(6):610-621.

[88] Paquis S, Legeay V, Konik H. Road Surface Classification by Thresholding Using Morphological Pyramid[C]. International Conference on Pattern Recognition, 2000, 1:334-337.

[89] Jain A K, Farrokhnia F. Unsupervised texture segmentation using Gabor filters[J]. Pattern Recognition, 1991, 24(12):1167-1186.

[90] Mallat S G. A theory for multiresolution signal decomposition: The wavelet representation[C]. IEEE transactions on Pattern Analysis and Macline Intelligence, 1989, 11:674-693.

[91] 肖旺新.路面破损图像自动识别关键技术研究[D].南京:东南大学,2004.

[92] 储江伟,初秀民,王荣本,等.沥青路面破损图像特征提取方法研究[J].中国图像图形学报,2003,8(10):1211-1217.

[93] Wang X, Feng X. Pavement distress detection and classification with automated image processing[C]. International Conference on Transportation, Mechanical, and Electrical Engineering, 2011:1345-1350.

[94] 孙奥.路面病害图像自动分类方法研究[D].南京:南京理工大学,2008.

[95] Song G Y, Lee K Y, Lee J W. Vehicle Detection by Edge-Based Candidate Generation and Appearence-based Classification [C]. IEEE Intelligent Vehicles Symposium, 2008:428-433.

[96] Ha D M, Lee J M, Kim Y D. Neural-edge-based vehicle detection and traffic parameter extraction[J]. Image and Vision Computing, 2004, 22(11):899-907.

[97] Wu J D, Liu C T. Finger-vein pattern identification using SVM and neural network technique [J]. Expert Systems with Applications, 2011, 38(11):14284-14289.

[98] Zhao C, Zhang B, Lian J, et al. Classification of driving postures by support vector machines [C]. Hefei: Image and Graphics (ICIG), 2011:926-930.

[99] Sun Z, Bebis G, Miller R. On-road vehicle detection using evolutionary Gabor filter optimization [J]. IEEE Transactions on Intelligent Transportation Systems, 2005, 6(4):125-137.

[100] Cheng H, Zheng N, Sun C. Boosted gabor features applied to vehicle detection [C]. The 18th International Conference on Pattern Recognition, 2006:662-666.

[101] Mario K. The curse of dimensionality [C]. The Fifth Online World Conference on Soft Computing in Industrial Applications (WSC5) Held on the Internet, 2000.

[102] Hespanha J P, Kriegman D. Eigenfaces vs. Fisherfaces: Recognition using class specific linear pro-

jection[J]. IEEE Transactions on Pattern Analysis and Machine Intelligence, 1997, 19(7):711-720.

[103] Sun Q, Zeng S, Liu Y P, et al. A new method of feature fusion and its application in image recognition[J]. Pattern Recognition, 2005, 38(12):2437-2448.

[104] Duda R O, Hart P E, Stork D G. Pattern Classification[M]. 2nd edition. New York: Wiley, 2001.

[105] Rodríguez J, Kuncheva L, Alonso C. Rotation forest: A new classifier ensemble method[J]. IEEE Transactions on Pattern Analysis and Machine Intelligence, 2006, 28(10):1619-1630.

[106] OpenCV(open source computer vision) wiki. http://opencv.willowgarage.com/wiki. Accessed on 1st June 2010.

[107] 沈花玉,王兆霞,高成耀,等. BP 神经网络隐含层单元的确定[C]. 天津理工大学学报,2008,24(5):13-15.

[108] Fu Y, Cao L, Guo G. Multiple feature fusion by subspace learning[C]. Proceedings of the 2008 international conference on Content-based image and video retrieval, Niagara Falls, Canada, 2008:127-134.

[109] Li Y, Gong P, Sasagawa T. Integrated shadow removal based on photogrammetry and image analysis[J]. International Journal of Remote Sensing, 2005, 26(18):3911-3929.

[110] Wu T P, Tang C K. A bayesian approach for shadow extraction from a single image[J]. Proc. of the International Conference on Computer Vision, 2005:480-487.

[111] Salvador E, Cavallaro A, Ebrahimi T. Cast shadow segmentation using invariant color features[J]. Computer Vision and Image Understanding, 2004, 95(2):238-259.

[112] 邹勤. 低信噪比路面裂缝增强与提取方法研究[D]. 武汉大学,2012.

[113] Donoho D L, Johnstone I M. Ideal spatial adaptation by wavelet shrinkage[J]. Biometrika, 1994, 81(3):425-455.

[114] Do M, Vetterli M. Contourlets: a directional multiresolution image representation [C]. New York: International Conference on Image Processing, 2002(1):357-360.

[115] Heusch G, Cardinaus F, Marcel S. Lighting normalization algorithms for face verification[J], Tech. Rep., IDIAP-Com, 2005,5(3):1-38.

[116] Dalal N, Triggs B. Histogram of oriented gradients for human detection[C]. IEEE Computer Society Conference on Computer Vision and Pattern Recognition, 2005(1):886-893.

[117] Bosch A, Zisserman A, Munoz X. Representing Shape with a Spatial Pyramid Kernel[C]. ACM International Conference on Image and Video Retrieval, 2007:401-408.

[118] Sikora. T. The MPEG-7 visual standard for content description-an overview[C]. IEEE Transactions on Circuits and Systems for Video Technology, 2011(11):696-702.

[119] Zhang P, Bui T D, Suen C Y. A novel cascade ensemble classifier system with a high recognition performance on handwritten digits[J]. Pattern Recognition, 2007, 40(12):3415-3429.

[120] Ranney T A, Mazzae E, Garrott R, Goodman M J. NHTSA driver distraction research: Past, present, and future. Transp. Res. Center Inc., East Liberty, OH, Tech. Rep., Jul. 2000.

[121] The Royal Society for the Prevention of Accidents. Driver fatigue and road accidents: A literature review and position. Birmingham, U.K., 2001.

[122] Croo H D, Bandmann, M Mackay G M, et al. The role of driver fatigue in commercial road transport crashes [R]. Eur. Transp. Safety Council, Brussels, Belgium, Tech. Rep., 2001.

[123] Lin C T, Wu R C, Liang S F, et al. EEG-based drowsiness estimation for safety driving using independent component analysis [J]. IEEE Trans. Circuits Syst. I, Reg. Papers, 2005, 52(12):

2726-2738.

[124] Lin C T, Chen Y C, Huang T Y, et al. Development of wireless brain computer interface with embedded multitask scheduling and its application on real-time driver's drowsiness detection and warning [J]. IEEE Trans. Biomed. Eng. , 2008, 55(5):1582-1591.

[125] Damousis I G, Tzovaras D. Fuzzy fusion of eyelid activity indicators for hypovigilance-related accident prediction [J]. IEEE Trans. Intell. Transp. Syst. , 2008, 9(3):491-500.

[126] Jap B T, Lal S, Fischer P, et al. Using EEG spectral components to assess algorithms for detecting fatigue [J]. Expert Syst. Appl. , 2009, 36(2):2352-2359.

[127] Yeo M V M, Li X P, Shen K. Can SVM be used for automatic EEG detection of drowsiness during car driving? [J]. Safety Sci. , 2009, 47(1):115-124.

[128] Hu S, Zheng G. Driver drowsiness detection with eyelid-related parameters by support vector machine [J]. Expert Syst. Appl. , 2009, 36(4):7651-7658.

[129] Liu J, Zhang C, Zheng C. EEG-based estimation of mental fatigue by using KPCA-HMM and complexity parameters [J]. Biomed. Signal Process. Control, 2010, 5(2):124-130.

[130] Yang G, Lin Y, Bhattacharya P. A driver fatigue recognition model based on information fusion and dynamic Bayesian network [J]. Inf. Sci. , 2010, 180(10):1942-1954.

[131] K Sibsambhu, B Mayank, R Aurobinda. EEG signal analysis for the assessment and quantification of driver's fatigue [J]. Transportation Research Part F Traffic Psychology and Behaviour, 2010, 13(5):297-306.

[132] Khushaba R N, Kodagoda S, L Sara, et al. Driver drowsiness classification using fuzzy wavelet-packet-based feature extraction algorithm [J]. IEEE Transactions on biomedical engineering, 2011, 58(1):121-131.

[133] Bergasa L, Nuevo J, Sotelo M, et al. Real-time system for monitoring driver vigilance [J]. IEEE Trans. Intell. Transp. Syst. , 2006, 7(1):63-77.

[134] Suzuki M, Yamamoto N, Yamamoto O, et al. Measurement of driver's consciousness by image processing—A method for presuming driver's drowsiness by eye-blinks coping with individual differences [C]. Proc. IEEE Int. Conf. Syst. , Man, Cybern. , 2007, 4:2891-2896.

[135] Orazio T D, Leo M, Guaragnella C. A visual approach for driver inattention detection [J]. Pattern Recognit. , 2007, 40(8):2341-2355.

[136] Friedrichs F, Yang B. Camera-based drowsiness reference for driver state classification under real driving conditions [J]. Proc. IEEE Intell. Veh. Symp. , 2010:101-106.

[137] Dong Y C, Hu Z C, Uchimura K, et al. Driver inattention monitoring system for intelligent vehicles: a review [J]. IEEE Transactions on Intelligent Transportation Systems, 2011, 12(2): 596-614.

[138] Eskandarian A, Sayed R, Delaigue P, et al. Advanced driver fatigue research [R]. U. S. Dept. Transp. , Fed. Motor Carrier Safety Admin. , Washington, DC, Tech. Rep. , Rep. 2007.

[139] Fan X, Sun Y, Yin B. Gabor-based dynamic representation for human fatigue monitoring in facial image sequences [J]. Pattern Recognit. Lett. , 2010, 31(3):234-243.

[140] Nadeau C L, Maag U, Bellavance F, et al. Wireless telephones and the risk of road crashes [J]. Accident Analysis and Prevention, 2003, 35(5):649-660.

[141] Liu X, Zhu Y D, Fujimura K. Real-time Pose Classification for Driver Monitoring [C]. Proceedings of the IEEE 5th International Conference on Intelligent Transportation Systems, Singapore, 2002:

174-178.

[142] Kato T, Fujii T, Tanimoto M. Detection of driver's posture in the car by using far infrared camera [J]. IEEE Intelligent Vehicles Symposium, Parma, Italy, 2004:339-344.

[143] Cheng S Y, Trivedi M M. Turn-Intent Analysis Using Body Pose for Intelligent Driver Assistance [J]. IEEE on Pervasive Computing, 2006, 5(4):28-37.

[144] Watta P, Lakshmanan S, Hou Y L. Nonparametric approaches for estimating driver pose [J]. IEEE Transactions on Vehicular Technology, 2007, 56(4):2028-2041.

[145] Cheng S Y, Park S, Trivedi M M. Multi-spectral and multi-perspective video arrays for driver body tracking and activity analysis [J]. Computer Vision and Image Understanding, 2007, 106(2-3): 245-257.

[146] Demirdjian D, Varri C. Driver poses estimation with 3D time-of-flight sensor [C]. IEEE Workshop on Computational Intelligence in Vehicles and Vehicular Systems, 2009:16-22.

[147] Yang C M, Wu C C, Chou C M, et al. Vehicle driver's ECG and sitting posture monitoring system [C]. Proceedings of the 9th International Conference on Information Technology and Applications in Biomedicine, Larnaca, Cyprus, 2009:1-4.

[148] Veeraraghavan H, Bird N, Atev S, et al. Classifiers for driver activity monitoring [J]. Transportation Research Part C: Emerging Technologies, 2007, 15(1):51-67.

[149] Paul V, Michael J J. Robust real-time face detection [J]. International Journal of Computer Vision, 2004, 57(2):137-154.

[150] Starck J, Candes E, Donoho D L. The curvelet transform for image denoising [J]. IEEE Transactions Image Processing, 2002, 11:670-684.

[151] Candes E, Donoho D L. Curvelets - A Surprisingly Effective Nonadaptive Representation for Objects with Edges. // Curves and Surfaces [M]. Vanderbilt University Press, 1999.

[152] Candes E L, Demanet D, Donoho L, et al. Fast discrete curvelet transforms [J]. Multiscale Modeling and Simulation, 2006, 5:861-899.

[153] Geback T, Koumoutsakos P. Edge detection in microscopy images using curvelets [J]. BMC Bioinformatics, 2009, 10:1-14.

[154] Sumana I, Islam M, Zhang D. Content based image retrieval using curvelet transform [C]. IEEE 10th Workshop on Multimedia Signal Processing, Cairns, Australia, 2008:11-16.

[155] Vapnik V N. Statistical Learning Theory [M]. New York: John Wiley & Sons, 1998.

[156] Platt J. Fast training of SVMs using sequential minimal optimization. // Advances in Kernel Methods Support Vector Machine [M]. Cambridge: MIT Press, 1999:185-208.

[157] KreBel U. Pairwise classification and support vector machines. // Advances in Kernel Methods: Support Vector Learning [M]. Cambridge: MIT Press, 1999.

[158] Milgram J, Cheriet M, Sabourin R. One against one or one against all: which one is better for handwriting recognition with SVMs? [C]. International Workshop on Frontiers in Handwriting Recognition, Montreal, Canada, 2006.

[159] Collins M. Discriminative training methods for hidden markov models: theory and experiments with perceptron algorithms [C]. Proceedings of Conferences on Empirical Methods in Natural Language Processing, Philadelphia, 2002, 10:1-8.

[160] Bremner D, Demaine E, Erickson J, et al. Output-sensitive algorithms for computing nearest-neighbor decision boundaries [J]. Discrete and Computational Geometry, 2005, 33(4):593-604.

[161] Simon H. Neural Networks: A Comprehensive Foundation (2ed.) [M]. Prentice Hall, 1998.

[162] Kraaijveld M A. A parzen classifier with an improved robustness against deviations between training and test data [J]. Pattern Recogn. Lett., 1996, 17(7):679-689.

[163] Zhang B L, Zhang Y C. Classification of cerebral palsy gait by kernel fisher discriminant analysis [J]. International Journal of Hybrid Intelligent Systems, 2008, 5(4):209-218.

[164] Cunha L, Zhou J P, Do M N. The nonsubsampled contourlet transform: theory, design, and applications [J]. IEEE Transactions on Image Processing, 2006,15(10): 3089-3101.

[165] Darrell S, Ed I. Nearest-Neighbor Methods in Learning and Vision [M]. MIT Press, 2005.

[166] Hall P, Park B U, Samworth R J. Choice of neighbor order in nearest-neighbor classification [J]. Annals of Statistics, 2008, 36(5):2135-2152.